One Faith, One Lord

A STUDY OF BASIC CATHOLIC BELIEF

Rev. Msgr. John F. Barry, P.A.

FIFTH EDITION

Sadlier

A Division of William H. Sadlier, Inc.

CONTENTS

Unit 1
Created and Saved

Unit 2
Welcomed into the Church

Unit 3
Eucharist & Reconciliation

Unit 4
Our Catholic Life

Living Our Faith

Our Catholic Roots

Imagine you are online, surfing the Internet. You find yourself at a Web site that poses many questions about human existence and the meaning of life. But the site does not answer these. Instead, it offers links that send you directly to Web sites of organizations, companies, universities, and publications that do attempt to answer such questions. What links might you expect to see on this Web site? What links would you add?

Our Catholic faith helps us to discover the meaning of life.

Human beings have always asked questions about the meaning of life and the origin of the world. No other creatures on earth can ask, "Where do things come from?" "Why are things the way they are?" or "What is the meaning of life?"

These are only some of the exciting questions that we can ask. For centuries, people have tried to answer such questions and to make sense out of life. They have tried to find satisfying answers in the following ways:

- reasoning, thinking, and generating ideas
- reflecting on their own experiences
- reaching out and exploring beyond everyday knowledge
- listening to those with whom they live and work.

All of these ways of discovery are wonderful—but they are limited. Reason and experience have never answered fully everything we need or want to know. They can only take us so far. We need something more. For Catholics, that something more is faith.

What is faith? Faith is not just another point of view. Faith is a gift from God. Faith helps us to begin to see our lives and the world as God sees them.

A person of faith knows that there is more to life than can be seen. Through the eyes of faith, we know that God is near, closer than we can imagine, and that God is the source of all life.

Faith, of course, does not take the place of reason, personal experience, human searching, or learning from others. Faith builds on our human abilities and works through them. We know this from experience. Throughout history, we see that some of the most creative and talented artists, educators, and scientists have been people of faith.

Faith is like a key that unlocks many doors. Our faith shows us answers we would most often be unable to discover by ourselves.

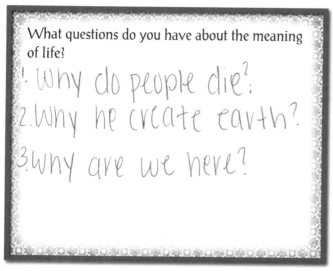

What questions do you have about the meaning of life?

1. Why do people die?

2. Why he create earth?

3. Why are we here?

② Through faith we come to know God.

Human beings have always used their reason to know that there must be some higher power at work in the world. When we look at ourselves and the universe around us, we realize that something so wonderful could not have come into existence or have happened by itself. So human beings search for an answer. They search for God.

In this search people living many thousands of years ago thought they had found the answer in nature. Some people named the gods they thought were at work in the terrifying clap of thunder, the flash of lightning, or the rumble of an earthquake. Others found their gods in the sun, moon, and stars.

You may know some of the fascinating stories and myths of ancient religions, such as those of Egypt, Greece, and Rome. In those religions, the gods were often pictured as animals or even as people, each in charge of some important part of life. But these creature-like gods were not the one true God. They did not satisfy the human search for the higher power at work in the world.

How does faith help you discover God in your life and in the world?

his love & forgiveness

The question still remained: Who really is God? The fullest answer to this question could only come from God. We call this Divine Revelation. The word *divine* is used to describe God, something that comes from God, or an expression of God. The word *revelation* means "the act of making someone or something known." This is why we call God's making himself known to us **Divine Revelation**.

At a chosen time in the history of the world, God wanted to make a special Revelation to human beings. He did this through the Israelites, the ancient Jews. Out of love God gradually revealed himself and his plan through words and deeds. Some of the things the Israelites came to know and believe about God were:

- There is only one true God, not many gods.

- God is not part of nature; he created nature and all that exists.

- God is a loving and caring God.

- God is active in the world and in our lives.

- We are called into a close relationship with God and called to live as God's people in the world.

We believe these things, too. But as Catholics we also believe that the one true God offered us his complete and full Revelation in Jesus Christ, his Son. Jesus Christ, the Son of God, shows us that God is Father, Son, and Holy Spirit. Our response to this Revelation is faith.

Faith is the gift from God by which we believe in God and all that he has revealed, and all that the Church proposes for our belief. We cannot earn faith. It is God's gift to us. By faith we can believe what God has shared about himself and his Creation. Yet even though God reveals himself, he remains a mystery.

Faith is also a personal act and a choice, a free response to God's Revelation of himself and his love for us.

Our faith is the faith of the Church. Just as we do not live alone, we do not believe alone. We try to live as persons of faith, especially by turning to God in prayer and worship. We also respond to God by living our faith and doing what he asks of us, taking care of ourselves, others, and the world around us.

7

In the Bible we read about God's relationship with our ancestors in faith.

The ancient Israelites were a nomadic people. Their wandering lifestyle did not allow them the time to record their special relationship with God or what God had revealed to them. Written documents were not even a part of their culture or way of life. But by word of mouth they passed on beautiful stories of faith, recounting in word and song all that God had done for them.

After many centuries the Israelites finally wrote down the oral traditions that had been passed from generation to generation. While the ancient authors chose their own words, expressions, and stories, they wrote under the guidance of the Holy Spirit. We call the special guidance that the Holy Spirit gave to the human authors of the Bible **Divine Inspiration**.

These writings were eventually collected in the book we call the **Bible**, or Scripture. The Bible is the written account of God's Revelation and his relationship with his people. The word *Bible* comes from Greek words meaning "books." The Bible is actually a collection of seventy-three smaller books divided into two main parts:

- The **Old Testament** contains forty-six books. In them we read about the faith relationship between God and the Israelites, later called the Jews.
- The **New Testament** contains twenty-seven books. They are about Jesus Christ, the Son of God, his message and mission, and his first followers.

The Bible was written over many centuries and had many human authors, all inspired by God. Because God inspired the human authors, he is also the author of the Bible. This is why all Scripture is the Word of God.

Do YOU Know?

God reveals himself to us through Scripture and Tradition. **Tradition** is the living transmission of the Word of God as entrusted to the Apostles and their successors by Jesus Christ and the Holy Spirit. It includes the Church's teachings, documents, worship, prayer, and other practices.

Catholics have deep respect for the Bible because it is God's Word to us. The Bible is a book about faith. It cannot be read as a science book or a modern history book. It is our most sacred book.

The human authors of the Bible used many different forms and styles of writing, including short stories, history, poetry, letters, and parables. Because the Bible was written so long ago and in so many different styles, we need to take time to study it carefully. Knowing the background of the human authors, the culture of the times, and the different forms and styles of writing helps us to better understand God's Word.

Belief in God's Word is a vital part of what it means to be a Catholic and to share in the beautiful faith life and tradition of our Church. What God did for our ancestors in faith, he continues to do for us.

What is the Bible? Why is it important to us?

GROWING IN FAITH

PRAY

As people of faith we turn to God in prayer. **Prayer** is talking and listening to God. We can pray alone, or we can join with others in communal prayer. In praising and thanking God for the gift of our lives, we also ask God for help because we trust in his love. Pray together:

✝ God be in my head,
and in my understanding;
God be in my eyes, and in my looking;
God be in my mouth, and in my speaking;
God be in my heart, and in my thinking;
God be in my end, and at my departing.

REFLECT & ACT

Faith must be alive! We cannot just talk about what we believe. We must live it.

What do people of faith do that is different from those who do not have faith? What can you do to grow in faith, to open your mind and heart to God?

REMEMBER
The Church teaches...

- ◎ Out of love, God has revealed himself and given himself to us. He has shared with us who he is and what he asks of us.

- ◎ Faith is both a gift from God and a free human act.

- ◎ Through faith and reason we have the ability to believe all that God reveals to us and to respond to God.

- ◎ The books of the Bible were written by human authors under the inspiration of the Holy Spirit.

- ◎ The Bible is divided into two parts, the Old Testament of forty-six books and the New Testament of twenty-seven books.

Faith Words

Divine Revelation (p. 7)
faith (p. 7)
Divine Inspiration (p. 8)
Bible (p. 8)
Old Testament (p. 8)
New Testament (p. 8)
Tradition (p. 8)
prayer (p. 9)

Think of someone you know and trust. What questions would you ask that person about the role faith has played in his or her life?

God the Creator

In his book <u>Brother Astronomer: Adventures of a Vatican Scientist</u>, Guy Consolmagna, S.J., wrote, "The mysteries of the quantum or the grandeur of the big bang aren't what give me faith. But as I see the pattern of creation unfolding ... I begin to get a closer appreciation of the personality of the Creator."

What questions do you have about Creation, faith, and the meaning of life?

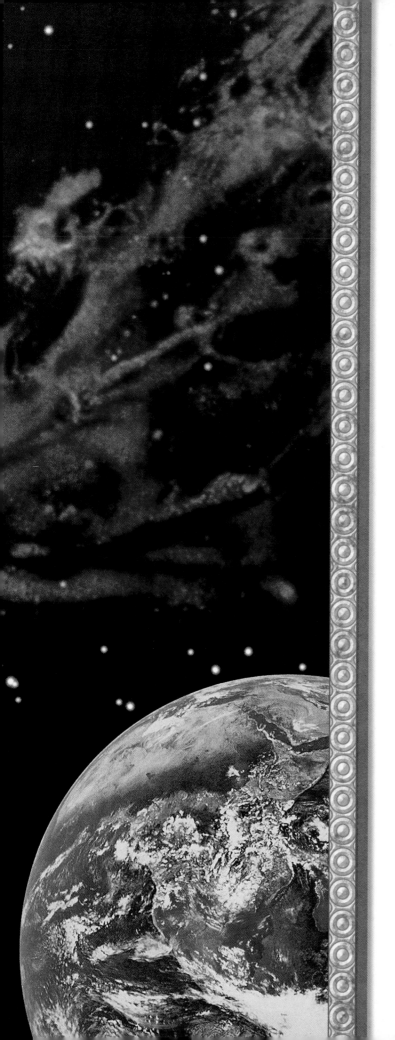

God is the Creator of the universe.

Every generation of people, young and old alike, tends to ask questions about the origin of the universe: Where did it come from? When did it start? How did it come into existence?

Scientists, historians, philosophers, and religious believers have all attempted to explain the origin of the universe. Scholars in many different areas of study have made unique and truthful contributions to our understanding of the origins of the universe. And research has raised even more questions.

People working in the fields of science and social studies try to answer important questions about how and when our world came into being. Over the centuries, as technology has advanced, our scientific theories about Creation have changed. Our knowledge has expanded.

But people do not just ask how and when. They also ask who and why: Who created the universe? Why was it created? Scientists ask where we came from, but as people of faith we also ask why we are here and where we are going. These questions can only be answered in faith.

In the Book of Genesis, the first book of the Bible, we find a beautiful and imaginative account of Creation. The Creation story is a simple, poetic story of the beginning of the universe. We read in the first Genesis account that God fashions the world in a spectacular way over a six-day period, the length of the ancient Israelites' workweek. The authors of Genesis show that God alone created everything. He begins by creating light. "Let there be light," he says (Genesis 1:3). And effortlessly—by the power of his word—God brings light into being.

Then, according to Genesis, God made the dome of the heavens—the sky. He gathered together the waters under the sky, causing dry land to appear. And "God called the dry land 'the earth,' and the basin of the water he called 'the sea.' God saw how good it was" (Genesis 1:10). On the seventh day, at the end of the workweek, the Genesis authors showed God doing just what the ancient Israelites did: resting after his labors.

From their description of Creation, we can see that the Genesis authors were not trying to answer questions of science, but questions of faith. For example, the word *day* found in the Creation account does not literally mean twenty-four hours. The seven days of Creation are simply the framework within which the Genesis authors tell the story.

Inspired by God and by the beauty and majesty of the world they saw around them, the authors wished to teach some important truths of faith:

- There is one and only one God.
- God alone created everything that is.
- God created the world and everything in it good.
- God created the world for his glory, out of his love and wisdom, and by his free choice.
- From the things God has made we can learn that he is all-powerful, all-loving, all-creative, and all-good.

> The Creation story is a wonderful one. Reflect on it. How does it help you to understand the existence of the universe?

Our faith helps us to know an equally important truth about Creation. It is that Creation is the work of God the Father, God the Son, and God the Holy Spirit. And Creation is kept in existence by God the Father, his Word—the Son, and the giver of life, the Holy Spirit.

 God is the Creator of all life.

In the imaginative account of Creation in the Book of Genesis, we read that God created all life: plants and trees, fish and birds, animals of every kind. Then, finally, God created humans, and made them in his own image and likeness:
"in the divine image he created him;
male and female he created them"
(Genesis 1:27).

No other creature or thing is made in the image of God. We are the crowning achievement of his Creation.

We all have **human dignity** which is the value and worth we share because God created us in his image and likeness. Because of this, each of us possesses an immortal **soul**, the invisible spiritual reality that makes each of us human and that will never die. Only human beings are capable of knowing and understanding themselves and their thoughts, feelings, and motivations. Only human beings can know and love God, and thus share in his life.

God calls each of us to a relationship with him, and we are able to respond in faith and love.

One significant way that the Israelites responded to their Creator was in prayer. A collection of these prayers, known as psalms, is contained in the Old Testament. The Book of Psalms contains many references to God as the Creator of everything, and to men and women as God's special Creation. We read in the psalms:

When I see your heavens, the work
  of your fingers,
  the moon and stars that you set
  in place—
What are humans that you are mindful
  of them,
  mere mortals that you care for them?
Yet you have made them little less than a
  god,
  crowned them with glory and honor.
Psalm 8:4–6

We alone have been given this gift of human dignity. Because of it we are free to love, to think, and to choose in God's likeness. God gives us the freedom to choose. This gift is called free will. We are responsible for our thoughts and actions. Being made in the image and likeness of God offers each of us a tremendous challenge.

> Explain what it means to you to be made in the image and likeness of God.

Do YOU Know?

Throughout the pages of the Bible, in both the Old and New Testaments, there are references to angels, or messengers from God. In fact, the word *angel* comes from the Greek word meaning "messenger." Angels were created by God as pure spirits without physical bodies. As you read the Bible, you will learn that angels are servants of God that help him to accomplish his mission of Salvation. The Church teaches that the angels watch over us and pray for us.

3 ## God calls us to share in the work of Creation.

Life is a gift. In a wondrous way, God created us male and female, partners with God and equal partners with each other.

You may be surprised to learn that in the Book of Genesis, chapters two and three, there is a second account of Creation. In this story about Creation, the Genesis authors introduce Adam and Eve as the first human beings. They represent all humanity. The authors of Genesis tell us that God spoke to Adam and Eve, saying, "Be fertile and multiply; fill the earth and subdue it. Have dominion over the fish of the sea, the birds of the air, and all the living things that move on the earth" (Genesis 1:28). These words help us to understand that God invites all of us to join him as partners in the work of and care for Creation.

God entrusted us with the care of Creation. God asks us to be **stewards of Creation**—to care for his Creation and to make sure that all people share in the goodness of Creation. God made the earth, the air, and the water for all his creatures to use. As God's stewards it is our responsibility to protect all the resources of the earth from destruction, pollution, or any sort of waste. To be effective partners with God, we must develop and use our talents and abilities. By improving our world, conserving its resources, and sharing what God has given us, we build a better life for all.

God's Creation is truly a wonder. But the work of Creation is not finished, and God calls us in many ways to assist him in his work of Creation. We can study agriculture and learn to sow better crops to feed the world's hungry. We can plant new trees to preserve the world's forests. We can build devices to filter water to keep our rivers and oceans clean. We can explore the surface of the earth, the depths of the oceans, and the vastness of space in search of things to benefit all humanity. By carrying out daily acts of stewardship, large and small, we make the glory of God's name known throughout all Creation.

Think of ways that you can be a partner with God in the work of Creation. Share your ideas.

GROWING IN FAITH

PRAY

The word *Amen* is a Hebrew word meaning "It is true!" or "So be it!" In the Mass and in all prayers, when we say "Amen" we are showing our agreement with what is being said. Pray together the following prayer.

✝ Blessed are you, O God,
Creator of the Universe,
who have made all things good
and given the earth for us to cultivate.
Grant that we may always use created
things gratefully
and share your gifts with those in need,
out of love of Christ our Lord,
who lives and reigns with you
for ever and ever.
Amen.

REFLECT & ACT

The authors of the Book of Genesis never could have dreamed that we would know as much about our world as we do today. They had no idea of the vast reaches of outer space or the marvelous microscopic world of the cell. But the lessons of faith they taught are still true.

What is it about Creation that leads you to think about God? Is there any time of the day that you are especially aware of God's creative power?

REMEMBER
The Church teaches...

- God created the universe. The scientific theory that the world was gradually formed over millions of years is compatible with Church teaching. Science and religion are partners in the search for truth.

- God made all the creatures of the universe, but human beings have a unique and special place in his Creation. God has created each person in his image with an immortal soul.

- From the things God has made we can learn that he is all-powerful, all-loving, all-creative, and all-good.

- God made us stewards of Creation, and we are called to respect and protect God's creatures and the environment.

- The gift of faith helps us to know that God is the source of all Creation.

Faith Words

human dignity (p. 13)
soul (p. 13)
stewards of Creation (p. 14)

How can people work together to protect and preserve the environment? Suggest some activities to help your parish, school, or neighborhood get involved in the care of Creation.

The Fall and the Promise

Our world is filled with people, places, and things that remind us of God's goodness. By their actions, thoughts, and beliefs, people choose to be and do good. However, evil and suffering do exist, and people suffer because of the evil actions of others. Have you ever wondered if the world was always like this? Why do you think suffering and evil exist?

① Evil and suffering entered the world through human choice.

We do not have to live very long to know that while life is filled with hope and joy, pain and disappointment are also part of life. Humans suffer from the effects of hatred, greed, and selfishness. The daily news is filled with reports of violence, suffering, and death, often brought about by human beings themselves.

Life is a mixture of good and bad. People may have high hopes; they also may have shattered dreams. People know happiness; they also experience sorrow.

Why is life both beautiful and tragic? The writers of the Book of Genesis asked the same puzzling question. As an answer, the authors, whom God inspired, tried to explain the origins of evil in the world. The Genesis authors wanted to teach us that evil has been part of the human experience since the very beginning.

In the second Creation account found in Genesis, the first man and woman, known as Adam and Eve, lived in and cared for a beautiful garden. The garden was God's gift to them. Adam and Eve did not suffer. They did not experience loneliness, pain, or worry. They lived in harmony with God, with each other, and with all of God's Creation. The Genesis authors wanted to show that God had created human beings to be in friendship with him, and in harmony with all of his Creation.

In the story God told Adam, "You are free to eat from any of the trees of the garden except the tree of knowledge of good and bad. From that tree you shall not eat; the moment you eat from it you are surely doomed to die" (Genesis 2:16–17).

Then the spirit of evil appeared. Disguised as a serpent, it spoke first to the woman, asking her whether God had really told her not to eat from any of the trees in the garden. The woman replied that God had told them they could eat the fruit of any tree except the tree in the middle of the garden. If they ate or touched the fruit from that tree, they would die. The serpent assured her that she would not die if she ate the fruit. In fact, the serpent said, as soon as she and Adam ate the fruit they would be like God and know what is good and what is bad.

The woman saw how beautiful the tree was and imagined how delicious its fruit would be to eat. She thought about how wonderful it would be to become like God. So she took the fruit and ate it. Then she gave some to Adam and he ate it, too.

By doing this, Adam and Eve rejected the wonderful gifts that God had given them. Through their own actions they chose evil over good. The Genesis authors wanted to show that evil and suffering had entered into our world through the human choice to disobey God. The man and the woman had broken their friendship with God and had lost the right to be with him in the garden. The authors showed this by having God send the couple away from the garden.

> What do you think led the first humans to make the choice they did in this story?
>
> *The fruit look good And it was a beautiful tree, she wanted to become like god.*

2 All of us suffer from the effects of Original Sin.

The story of Adam and Eve taught very important truths of faith. It was the kind of dramatic story that was easy for the ancient Israelites to remember and understand. It was built on symbols that were very familiar to them.

The Genesis authors wanted to show God's love for the first human beings by placing them in a garden filled with running water, lush plants, and trees filled with fruit. To the Israelites, who had been living in or near a desert, the garden was a symbol of happiness and of God's grace. **Grace** is a participation, or a sharing, in God's life and friendship. This free and undeserved gift of grace introduces us into the life of the Most Blessed Trinity and helps us to respond to God's call to become his children.

The garden is not the only symbol in the story of Adam and Eve. The Genesis authors used objects and actions as symbols as well:

- To the Israelites, the serpent was a symbol of evil. The Israelites worshiped only the one true God. Their pagan neighbors, however, often worshiped serpents.

- Hearing that Adam and Eve chose to eat the fruit of the forbidden tree helped the Israelites to appreciate the power they had as human beings to choose between good and evil.

- Adam and Eve's being sent out of the garden reflected the consequences of turning away from God and the loss of God's grace.

The story of the garden dramatizes how close the relationship is between God and humans. But it also tells us about the shattering of that relationship.

Adam and Eve did not respond gratefully or lovingly to God. They gave into temptation because they thought their choice would bring them happiness. Adam and Eve turned away from God, selfishly choosing what they wanted rather than what God wanted for

them. This story depicts the first sin committed by the first human beings. We call this sin **Original Sin**. Every person is born with Original Sin. Because of Original Sin, each one of us is inclined to sin, and each of us is subject to ignorance, suffering, and death. The effects of Original Sin challenge us throughout life.

This simple story from Genesis offers much truth about our relationship with God and our need to be brought back into the life of grace.

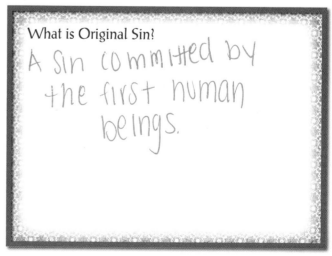

What is Original Sin?

A Sin committed by the first human beings.

19

God promised to send the world a Savior.

The Genesis story of Adam and Eve did not end in despair. It ended on a note of hope and mercy. The inspired authors of Genesis knew that God would never abandon human beings. In the story God had promised that sin and evil would not triumph, that the offspring of Adam and Eve would one day win over evil.

The Israelites knew that the journey back to a full and loving relationship with God was going to be a difficult one. Even though people would still sin, God would forgive them and never stop loving them.

When the Israelites felt low and hopeless, God encouraged them. He sent special people called prophets to speak for him and to remind people that he had not forgotten them. Through the prophets, God called Israel and all nations to turn to him. He promised to send them the Messiah, the Anointed One, who would restore their relationship with God. God fulfilled his promise by sending his own Son to us.

Those who first followed Christ identified him as the "New Adam"—the new Man. They believed that Jesus Christ was the Son of God who came into the world and brought victory over evil and sin. Through his obedience to God the Father unto death, Jesus Christ became the Savior of the world. Through Jesus, we are restored to God's life and love. Faith is our necessary response to the Salvation that Jesus has won for us.

The New Testament tells us about the life of Jesus, his Death on the cross, and his being raised from the dead. Through his suffering, Death, and Resurrection, Jesus Christ saves us from evil and shares God's life and love in a human way. The Church calls the suffering, Death, Resurrection, and Ascension of Jesus Christ the **Paschal Mystery**; by this great mystery of faith we are redeemed. We celebrate this great mystery each time we gather for the celebration of the Mass.

How would you explain to a younger person that God fulfilled his promise?

GROWING IN FAITH

PRAY

Just as God called us into being, he continually calls us to meet him through prayer. In prayer we respond to that call, and we raise our hearts and minds to God. Silently reflect on the following prayer:

✝ God our Creator,
You created all people out of love.
You judge us fairly and with justice,
but in mercy you redeem us
through Jesus Christ our Lord.
Amen.

REMEMBER
The Church teaches...

◉ God created humans to be in friendship with him and in harmony with each other and with all Creation.

◉ Sin entered the world through human choice.

◉ The first sin committed by the first human beings is called Original Sin. Every human being is born with Original Sin and suffers from its effects.

◉ Jesus Christ is the "New Adam" whose obedience even to death saves us from sin.

◉ Jesus Christ fulfills all God's promises and frees us to share in God's life and love.

Faith Words

grace (p. 18)
Original Sin (p. 19)
Paschal Mystery (p. 20)

REFLECT & ACT

What evidence of Original Sin can you find in today's headlines and news stories? Could any of these situations have been avoided?

What can you do to lessen pain and evil in the world? What actions can you take to share the Christian belief that Jesus is a sign of hope?

The Promise Fulfilled

What do you think the phrase "God works in mysterious ways" means?

 ## God sent his only Son to us.

Over many centuries God prepared the people of Israel for the fulfillment of his promises. Little by little he revealed, through the words of the prophets, some insight into the Promised One to come. The prophets foretold that the Promised One would be from the family of David, the greatest king of Israel. He would be born in Bethlehem. He would be called God's Anointed One, the Messiah.

Knowing the message of the prophets, the first Christians could see that Jesus Christ fulfilled the prophets' words. The early Christians preached this Good News. Some were inspired by the Holy Spirit to record their beliefs and experiences in the pages of what we now know as the New Testament.

We read in the New Testament that over two thousand years ago God sent an angel to a young Jewish girl who lived in the town of Nazareth. Her name was Mary, and she was promised in marriage to a man named Joseph. After greeting her, the angel said, "Do not be afraid, Mary, for you have found favor with God. Behold, you will conceive in your womb and bear a son, and you shall name him Jesus. He will be great and will be called Son of the Most High" (Luke 1:30–32).

Because she had not had relations with a man, Mary questioned the angel. And then the angel told her something astonishing: "The holy Spirit will come upon you, and the power of the Most High will overshadow you. Therefore the child to be born will be called holy, the Son of God" (Luke 1:35). Mary totally accepted what God wanted her to do. She told the angel, "Behold, I am the handmaid of the Lord. May it be done to me according to your word" (Luke 1:38).

23

We call the angel's visit to Mary and the announcement that she would be the virgin mother of the Son of God the **Annunciation**. The example of Mary's "yes" to God inspires us to work with her son as she did. Since Mary is the Mother of God and Mother of the Church, we lovingly call her Blessed Mother.

Luke chose to record the events of the Annunciation in his Gospel. This is an important indicator that the first Christians believed that God had fulfilled his promise in a way that no one had expected. The Promised One was not only a great man, he was God's own Son as well.

Why do you think Mary responded as she did to God's message? Would it be hard for you to respond as Mary did? Why or why not?

Jesus Heals a Sick Boy, Frank Ordaz

② Jesus Christ is true God and true man.

Where do we discover the truth about Jesus—about who he really is? The writings of the New Testament proclaim the Good News of Jesus Christ. The word *gospel* means "good news." The **Gospels** are the accounts of God's Revelation through Jesus Christ. The Gospels of Matthew, Mark, Luke, and John have a central place in Scripture because they are all about the Good News of Jesus. These four accounts were written after the Death and Resurrection of Jesus. They are God's Word, and they also express the faith of the early Church community.

Although they are not biographies, the Gospels are a rich source of information about Jesus. They give us a stirring picture of Jesus' humanity—who he was and what he did:

- Jesus was the son of Mary.
- He obeyed his parents, prayed, and visited the Temple.
- He labored as a carpenter, enjoyed friendship, and felt emotions like sadness, happiness, anger, and love.
- He suffered and died.

The friends of Jesus traveled the same roads as he did, sharing his joys and sorrows. Jesus' friends did not doubt that he was human, just as they were. But Jesus dared to say and do things only God could do:

- He healed the sick, restored sight to the blind, and brought the dead back to life.

24

- He calmed raging seas. He fed thousands with a small amount of food that was meant to serve only a few.

- He forgave people's sins.

Through such words and deeds his followers came to know that Jesus was more than a mere man: Jesus was divine.

Jesus himself expressed his divinity clearly when he spoke about God his Father. One day Jesus asked his followers: "Do you not believe that I am in the Father and the Father is in me?" (John 14:10). Jesus was also establishing his own identity when he said, "The Father and I are one" (John 10:30). We learn from the very first chapter

Jesus Calms the Stormy Sea, Frank Ordaz

of John's Gospel one of the great truths of our faith: Jesus is the Word of God, and the Word became flesh, taking on our human nature and dwelling among us. The **Incarnation** is the truth that the Son of God, the second Person of the Blessed Trinity, became man and lived among us in order to accomplish our Salvation.

From its beginning the Church has continually searched for a deeper understanding of Jesus. In the early days of the Church, disputes about Jesus' nature arose. Some people began to teach that Jesus was only a man. Others taught that he was the Son of God but not fully human.

In the fifth century all the bishops met to discuss the issue of Jesus' humanity and divinity. With the guidance of the Holy Spirit, the bishops proclaimed this great truth of faith: Jesus Christ is true God and true man. This means that Jesus is both fully human and fully divine.

Do YOU Know?

We learn from the Gospels of Luke and Matthew that God's promises were fulfilled in the birth of Jesus. However, in Matthew's Gospel the story is told from Joseph's perspective rather than Mary's. In this Gospel we read that an angel came to Joseph in a dream and spoke these assuring words: "Joseph, son of David, do not be afraid to take Mary your wife into your home. For it is through the holy Spirit that this child has been conceived in her. She will bear a son and you are to name him Jesus, because he will save his people from their sins" (Matthew 1:20–21). The very name *Jesus* means "God saves."

What do we mean by the Incarnation? What does it tell us about the humanity and divinity of Christ?

He was divine because

3 Jesus teaches us about God and the Kingdom of God.

Jesus' followers knew about and believed in the one true God. But Jesus taught them more. Jesus taught them about God his Father, and he spoke to his followers about the Holy Spirit: "The Advocate, the holy Spirit that the Father will send in my name—he will teach you everything and remind you of all that [I] told you" (John 14:26).

We learn from Jesus that God is Father, Son, and Holy Spirit. This teaching of Jesus' does not mean that there are three gods. It means that there are three Divine Persons in one God: the Father, the Son, and the Holy Spirit. This is what we call the **Blessed Trinity**:

- God the Father is the first Person of the Blessed Trinity.
- God the Son is the second Person of the Blessed Trinity.
- God the Holy Spirit is the third Person of the Blessed Trinity.

God is one community of three Divine Persons, and these three are one and share a single mission.

Some people ask, "How can there be three Persons in one God?" This is a matter of faith. It is, in fact, the central mystery of our faith, revealed in the Incarnation and in the sending of the Holy Spirit. Belief in the Blessed Trinity is at the very root of our faith. We celebrate the relationship of Father, Son, and Holy Spirit in our prayer and in our worship. We can see this most particularly in our Baptism: We are all baptized in the name of the Father, and of the Son, and of the Holy Spirit.

Jesus told us more about God in his teaching on the Kingdom of God. Jesus spoke constantly about the Kingdom, or Reign, of God. He invited us all to enter the Kingdom, to follow God's will through our words and deeds.

Jesus never defined the Kingdom of God. Instead, he used beautiful stories called parables to describe the Kingdom, how important it is, and how it grows. Many of these parables begin with the words, "the kingdom of heaven is like. . . ." In the thirteenth chapter of Matthew's Gospel, we read that the Kingdom can be compared to:

- a tiny seed that will blossom into a large bush
- the yeast that makes bread rise
- a buried treasure or a pearl of great price
- a net thrown into the sea that collects fish of every kind.

The Kingdom of God is not a place or a political state. **The Kingdom of God** is the power of God's love active in our lives and in our world. Through his teaching, his miracles, and his healing ministry, Jesus brought about God's Kingdom in a unique way. Jesus himself is the Good News of God's Kingdom—a Kingdom that is here now and yet is growing until the end of time. We believe that the Church is the seed and beginning of the Kingdom of God on earth.

Describe the Kingdom of God in your own words.

GROWING IN FAITH

PRAY

The priest's greeting to the gathered assembly at Mass expresses our relationship to the Trinity in this way: "The grace of our Lord Jesus Christ, and the love of God, and the communion of the Holy Spirit be with you all." Our prayer, both personal and communal, draws us into the life of the Trinity. Pray together:

✝ Glory to the Father,
and to the Son,
and to the Holy Spirit:
as it was in the beginning, is now,
and will be for ever.
Amen.

REFLECT & ACT

What does Jesus' teaching on the Kingdom of God mean for us? When we follow Jesus, when we live by his example and are guided by the Holy Spirit, we help to build God's Kingdom. We are called to bring God's love to the world, to all people, and to all Creation.

Think of some things you can do to further the Kingdom of God on earth.

REMEMBER

The Church teaches...

◎ The Blessed Virgin Mary conceived by the power of the Holy Spirit and gave birth to the Son of God.

◎ The Blessed Trinity is the three Divine Persons in one God: the Father, the Son, and the Holy Spirit.

◎ God the Father is the first Person of the Blessed Trinity; God the Son is the second Person of the Blessed Trinity; God the Holy Spirit is the third Person of the Blessed Trinity.

◎ Jesus Christ is the Son of God, the second Person of the Blessed Trinity who became one of us. He is true God and true man.

◎ The Kingdom of God is the power of God's love active in our lives and in our world. It is present now and will come in its fullness at the end of time.

Faith Words

Annunciation (p. 24)
Gospels (p. 24)
Incarnation (p. 25)
Blessed Trinity (p. 26)
Kingdom of God (p. 26)

How would you explain to a friend the Church teaching that Jesus is both fully human and fully divine?

CHAPTER 5

Jesus, the Savior

Filipino teenager Pedro Calungsod was working with a Spanish Jesuit missionary on the island of Guam. Pedro was glad to be doing what he believed God wanted of him. On April 2, 1672, when they were teaching some people about Jesus, Pedro and a priest were killed by local men who hated Christians. Why would a teenager be willing to risk his or her life to do God's work? Do you know of any teenager who tries to teach about Jesus?

① Jesus faithfully did the work God his Father gave him.

One of the central beliefs of the people of Old Testament times was that of a **Messiah**—a person God planned to send to save the people from their sins. God fulfilled his promise by sending his own Son, Jesus Christ, to be the Savior and Messiah. In the time that Jesus lived on earth, there was a great deal of speculation about when this Messiah, or Savior, would come and what he would be like. Authors of the books of the Old Testament had described the Messiah as anointed king, just ruler, liberator, and Savior. He would restore Israel to its rightful place as a kingdom ruled only by God and influential over other nations.

Most Jews hoped for a powerful king who would free Israel from domination by foreigners and bring prosperity to the people. The symbol of this new kingdom was a great banquet at which the king would preside and the people of Israel would celebrate their victory over their oppressors. For this reason many of the people were not prepared for the kingdom that Jesus announced.

According to the Gospels a large crowd often followed Jesus, but Jesus was never controlled by the whims of the crowd. When they wanted to make him king, Jesus fled. When they asked him, "Are you the one who is to come or should we look for another?" (Matthew 11:3), Jesus answered by using the words of the prophet Isaiah to describe the time of the Messiah: "The blind regain their sight, the lame walk, lepers are cleansed, the deaf hear, the dead are raised, and the poor have the good news proclaimed to them" (Matthew 11:5).

From the Gospel accounts we learn that early Christians believed that Jesus was the Messiah. The word *messiah* comes from the Hebrew word for "anointed." In the New

29

Testament, which was written in Greek, the word *christos* was used to translate *messiah*. In English this word is *Christ*. The titles Messiah, Christ, and Anointed One all mean the same thing. We call Jesus—Christ, Messiah, and Anointed One.

Jesus did not deny that he was the Messiah, but Jesus was not the kind of Messiah that the people expected. His mission was not directed toward himself or earthly kingship and prosperity, but toward his Father. The Son of God came to earth to do his Father's will: to save us from sin and unite us with himself so that we could share in God's life and love. We read in the Gospel of John that Jesus describes himself as "the way and the truth and the life. No one comes to the Father except through me" (John 14:6).

Jesus' friends realized how faithfully he had done God's will by denying himself and serving the needs of all. All of Jesus' life was a constant teaching. He:

- fed the hungry and helped the poor
- forgave sinners and healed the sick
- taught people about God and what he asked of them
- called all people, women and men alike, to share God's life and love.

The followers of Jesus would have to obey God's will as Jesus himself did in order to become disciples. A **disciple** is one who says yes to Jesus' call to follow him. All were welcome, but they would have to put aside selfishness to become disciples.

> Did Jesus fit the people's idea of the Messiah? Why or why not?

 Jesus died on the cross for us.

Jesus was completely faithful to God and to the customs and laws of his people. But Jesus dared to interpret the Law of Moses with divine authority. Such acts brought him into conflict with the religious and civil leaders of his time.

In Mark's Gospel we read that Jesus predicted that certain leaders would put him to death, but that he would rise three days later. One of Jesus' followers took him aside and urged him to see things as others did. But Jesus told his disciple that God's thinking is not like ours.

All four Gospels record the details of Jesus' Passion—his suffering and Death. Jesus and his disciples had traveled to Jerusalem for the Jewish Feast of Passover. Every year faithful Jews of Jesus' time—as well as those

Christ Healing the Withered Hand, James J. Tissot, circa 1870

today—prepared a special meal to celebrate God's delivering them from slavery in Egypt. Jesus knew that this would be his last Passover meal because he would be betrayed.

At what we now call the Last Supper, Jesus taught his disciples about love and promised them that the Father would send the Holy Spirit. Jesus went with his disciples to pray in the Garden of Olives, a beautiful garden on a hill overlooking the city of Jerusalem. There Jesus agonized over his coming death. He fell to the ground and prayed, "My Father, if it is possible, let this cup pass from me; yet, not as I will, but as you will" (Matthew 26:39).

Jesus' fear of death was very real, but his faith was rooted in his Father. He was able to face suffering and death knowing how much his Father loved him. While Jesus prayed in the garden, he was betrayed by his disciple Judas. Jesus was then arrested and brought to trial, and his other disciples deserted him, fleeing from the area.

Jesus was brought before Pontius Pilate, the Roman governor of Judea. Pilate asked Jesus whether he was the king of the Jews. Pilate knew that Jesus did not claim to be an earthly king, but Pilate still believed that any talk of kingship was a threat to Roman authority. So Jesus was condemned to die.

The Roman soldiers led Jesus to the place where he would be crucified. Crucifixion was a form of execution the Romans used for common criminals. Jesus did not struggle, protest, or resist as he was nailed to the cross. With trust and love he placed his life in his Father's care: "Father, into your hands I commend my spirit" (Luke 23:46). Jesus said this and died. Good Friday is the name we give to the day Jesus died for us.

The Agony in the Garden (Christ in the Garden of Olives),
Paul Gauguin, 1889

How did Jesus' determination to do the will of his Father affect his disciples?

Do YOU Know?

We learn from many religious and political situations today that an entire nation, people, or religious group cannot be held responsible for the actions of some of its members. Blessed Pope John Paul II reminded us of this during his visit to a Roman synagogue in 1986. The Pope stated that in no way can Christians blame "the Jews as a people for what happened in Christ's passion."

Resurrection Icon, Sophie Hacker/Bridgeman Art Library

 By rising from the dead, Jesus Christ brings us new life.

For a short time Jesus' Death crushed the disciples' hopes that he was their Messiah. The disciples hid for fear of death or imprisonment because of their association with Jesus. Then, as the Gospels record it, the unexpected happened. Some women followers of Jesus went to his burial place, expecting to anoint his body. But the large stone at the tomb's entrance had been rolled away. The tomb was empty!

The women's first thoughts were that someone had stolen the body. Then they saw an angel robed in white and became frightened. The angel told them, "Do not be afraid! I know that you are seeking Jesus the crucified. He is not here, for he has been raised just as he said. Come and see the place where he lay" (Matthew 28:5–6).

The women were amazed, and they ran to tell the disciples. As they made their way, the risen Jesus met them. He spoke to them, and they honored him by embracing his feet. When the women told the disciples what they had seen and heard the disciples did not believe.

Later, on the day we now celebrate as Easter Sunday, the risen Jesus appeared to his disciples. Even though they were behind locked doors, Jesus came among them and said, "Peace be with you" (John 20:19). Jesus' disciples were filled with joy at seeing their Lord among them, truly risen from the dead.

After Jesus' **Resurrection**, the mystery of Jesus' rising from Death to new life, the empty tomb and Christ's appearances as the Risen One awakened the disciples' faith in the power of God. We share the disciples' faith that Jesus is risen. Jesus' Resurrection is a central belief of our faith. Because of his Resurrection Jesus' life and death have meaning. The power of sin and evil was broken for all time.

Through his Death Christ opened the gates of Heaven and freed us from the power of sin and evil. By his Resurrection we are restored to new life. Through Jesus Christ humanity was reunited with God. As Saint Paul reminds us, "For just as in Adam all die, so too in Christ shall all be brought to life" (1 Corinthians 15:22).

> Why is belief in the Resurrection of Jesus Christ so important to our faith?

GROWING IN FAITH

PRAY

The Easter joy of Jesus' Resurrection is captured in one word—*Alleluia*. The word *Alleluia* comes from the Hebrew for "Praise the Lord!" The Alleluia is most often used as an acclamation. Pray together:

✝ Jesus Christ
is risen from the dead,
Alleluia!

REMEMBER

The Church teaches...

◉ Jesus' mission was directed toward his Father. He came to do his Father's will.

◉ Jesus is the Messiah, the promised Savior. *Messiah* is a word that means "Christ," or the Anointed One of God. That is why we say that Jesus is the Christ.

◉ Jesus died to save us from sin, and his Resurrection restores us to new life.

◉ The Resurrection of Jesus is a central belief of our faith. We share the belief of the first disciples that Jesus is risen.

Faith Words

Messiah (p. 29)
disciple (p. 30)
Resurrection (p. 32)

REFLECT & ACT

Jesus did the will of the Father despite opposition. Do you know anyone who did what he or she believed was right in spite of opposition? What consequences did the action have for that person?

In what ways can you live out the meaning of the life of Jesus? What can you do to share the hope of Jesus' Resurrection with others?

A. Choose the correct term to complete each statement.

Incarnation	Grace	stewards of Creation
Resurrection	Divine Revelation	Blessed Trinity
Gospels	Original Sin	Paschal Mystery
Old Testament	Kingdom of God	New Testament
Messiah	Faith	Annunciation

1. The _____ is the mystery of Jesus' rising from Death to new life.

2. The first sin committed by the first human beings is known as _____.

3. Those who take care of everything that God has given them are called _____.

4. _____ is the gift from God by which we believe in God and all that he has revealed, and all that the Church proposes for our belief.

5. _____ is God's making himself known to us.

6. In the _____ we read about the faith relationship between God and the Israelites.

7. The _____ is the person God planned to send to save people from their sins.

8. The _____ is the three Divine Persons in one God: God the Father, God the Son, and God the Holy Spirit.

9. The accounts found in the New Testament of God's Revelation through Jesus Christ are known as the _____ .

10. The _____ is the power of God's love active in our lives and in our world, which is present now and will come in its fullness at the end of time.

11. The _____ is the truth that the Son of God, the second Person of the Blessed Trinity, became man and lived among us in order to accomplish our Salvation.

12. _____ is a participation, or sharing, in God's life and friendship.

13. The _____ refers to the suffering, Death, Resurrection, and Ascension of Jesus Christ.

14. The _____ is the name given to the announcement to Mary that she would be the Mother of the Son of God.

15. In the second part of the Bible, the _____, we read about Jesus Christ, his message and mission, and his first followers.

B. Circle the response that does *not* belong.

1. Our Catholic faith helps us
   a. discover the meaning of life.
   b. have all the answers.
   c. come to know God.
   d. give a free response to God's Revelation of himself.

2. This is what the Church teaches about the fall and the promise:
   a. evil and suffering entered the world through human choice.
   b. Jesus Christ fulfills God's promise to free human beings to share in God's life.
   c. every human being suffers the effects of Original Sin.
   d. the first humans did not sin.

3. From the Book of Genesis we learn that
   a. Creation was completed in seven years.
   b. God alone created everything that is.
   c. the world God created is good.
   d. we are made in the image and likeness of God.

4. We find in the four Gospel accounts that Jesus
   a. worked no miracles.
   b. is the Son of God and the long-awaited Messiah.
   c. is both divine and human.
   d. is one with the Father.

5. Jesus fulfilled his Father's will by
   a. feeding the hungry and healing the sick.
   b. suffering and dying on the cross.
   c. avoiding contact with the poor.
   d. rising from the dead to bring us new life.

C. Share your faith by responding thoughtfully to these questions.

1. How does your faith make a difference in your life? How can you strengthen your faith?

   _____

   _____

2. In what ways can you live out your responsibility to take care of Creation?

   _____

   _____

3. What meaning do these symbols from the story of Adam and Eve have for you?

   the garden: _____

   _____

   the serpent: _____

   _____

   being sent from the garden: _____

   _____

4. Why is it important to help build up the Kingdom of God? What can you do to spread the Kingdom?_____

   _____

5. How does the suffering and Death of Jesus help you to cope with the sorrows in your own life? Why does Jesus' Resurrection give you hope?

   _____

   _____

Jesus Sends the Holy Spirit

Sister Ita Ford wrote to her niece, "I hope you come to find that which gives life a deep meaning for you. Something worth living for—maybe even worth dying for—something that energizes you, enthuses you, enables you to keep moving ahead." Have you ever experienced a time when you were motivated and energized by someone or something? Did the feeling last?

 Jesus promised to send the Holy Spirit.

We all need vision and goals to give us direction. We need courage and hope and someone to help guide us if we get off track. Jesus has given these things to us in a way we never could have imagined.

Jesus provided a sense of purpose, strength, and direction for his followers. His presence among his disciples, his teachings, and his way of life united them. Among these followers were a special group we know as the *Apostles*, a word meaning "those sent on a mission." The **Apostles** were twelve men chosen by Jesus to share in his mission in a special way.

Jesus promised his Apostles that he would be with them always. He would do this by sending the Holy Spirit to guide and encourage them. Jesus assured his Apostles with these words, "You will receive power when the holy Spirit comes upon you, and you will be my witnesses in Jerusalem, throughout Judea and Samaria, and to the ends of the earth" (Acts of the Apostles 1:8). The Holy Spirit would help them find the way to bring Jesus' message of God's love to the entire world.

Jesus told his Apostles, "When the Advocate comes whom I will send you from the Father, the Spirit of truth. . . . he will testify to me. And you also testify, because you have been with me from the beginning" (John 15:26–27). The **Advocate** is God the Holy Spirit, the third Person of the Blessed Trinity. The Holy Spirit would:

- remain with them and in them
- teach them and help them to remember all that Jesus had said

③ The Holy Spirit helped the disciples to be Christ's witnesses.

Peter's proclamation of Jesus as Lord was very powerful. Lord was a title reserved only for God, and Peter truly believed in Jesus' divinity. Peter told the people gathered, "Repent and be baptized, every one of you, in the name of Jesus Christ for the forgiveness of your sins; and you will receive the gift of the holy Spirit" (Acts of the Apostles 2:38).

The Holy Spirit was at work through the Apostles. Through the power of the Holy Spirit, thousands of people changed their lives:

- They were baptized.
- Their sins were forgiven.
- They shared in the Gift of the Holy Spirit.
- The Holy Spirit made them one in their love for God and one another.

We read in the Acts of the Apostles about the way the early Christians tried to live. They committed themselves to the Apostles' teachings about Jesus. They lived together in fellowship and prayer. The early Christians ate together and shared their possessions. They cared for the needy as best they could. In what they said and what they did, they were witnesses of Jesus Christ.

To witness is to provide evidence for or to testify to the truth or validity of something. The word *witness* means "someone who has seen or heard something, or someone who gives evidence." This word brings up images of an eyewitness to a crime or a character witness in a court hearing. Being a witness or giving witness in these situations is not a life long task. But being a life long witness is exactly what Jesus calls us to. **Witnesses** are people who speak and act based upon what they know and believe about Jesus Christ.

To be a Christian is not just to believe in Jesus Christ. We must give witness to Christ in all that we say and do. We need to share the Good News of Jesus with others. When people see us, they should see the power of Christ in our lives. If they do, they may come to believe, too.

The Apostles were the first witnesses of Jesus—they saw, touched, and spoke with him. The early Christians were called to give witness to the life and mission of Jesus. Many practiced their faith in spite of persecution from the government and from people who were not Christians.

We, too, are called to be Christ's witnesses through the actions, words, and thoughts of our daily lives. Sometimes this requires courage; sometimes it requires sacrifice; but through it all the Holy Spirit is with us, assisting us in living as followers of Jesus Christ.

> Describe someone who is a true witness to Christ's life and teachings.

Growing in Faith

PRAY

Jesus prayed at all times of the day. He asked his Father's blessing before he acted, and he thanked his Father afterward. Jesus prayed for strength and direction, and he taught his disciples to do the same. Jesus told them, "Ask and you will receive; seek and you will find; knock and the door will be opened to you" (Luke 11:9).

✝ Breathe into me Holy Spirit,
that my thoughts may be all holy.
Move in me, Holy Spirit,
that my work too, may be holy.
Attract my heart, Holy Spirit,
that I may love only what is holy.
Strengthen me, Holy Spirit,
that I may defend all that is holy.
Protect me, Holy Spirit,
that I always may be holy.
Amen.

REMEMBER
The Church teaches...

- ◉ God the Holy Spirit is the third Person of the Blessed Trinity.

- ◉ The Apostles were twelve men chosen by Jesus to share in his mission in a special way.

- ◉ Jesus Christ sent his disciples the Gift of the Holy Spirit.

- ◉ The Holy Spirit is the Advocate: the helper, consoler, and teacher who strengthens and guides us.

- ◉ The Holy Spirit is in us and with us at all times, drawing us together as God's people, making the Church one in truth and love.

Faith Words

Apostles (p. 37)
Advocate (p. 37)
Pentecost (p. 39)
witnesses (p. 40)

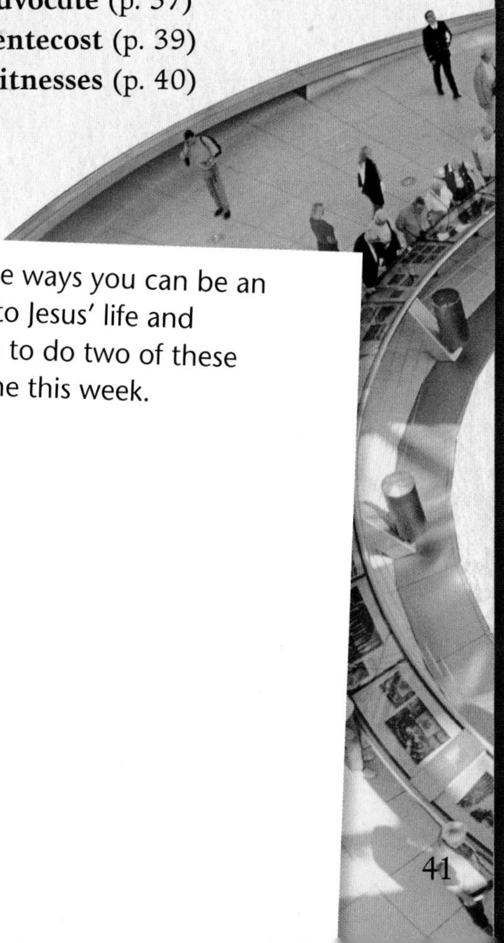

REFLECT & ACT

Do you prefer to think of the Holy Spirit as a helper, teacher, consoler, or defender? Why? When you are in need of help, do you ever ask the Holy Spirit to guide or help you?

Think about the ways you can be an active witness to Jesus' life and teachings. Plan to do two of these things sometime this week.

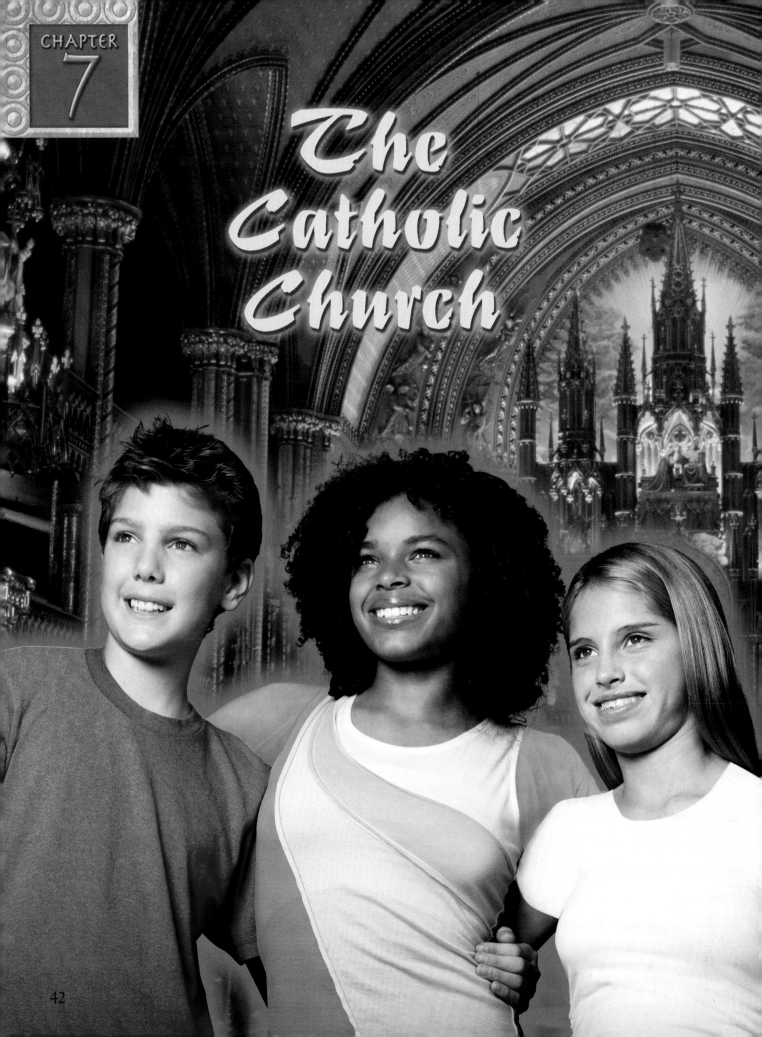

CHAPTER 7

The Catholic Church

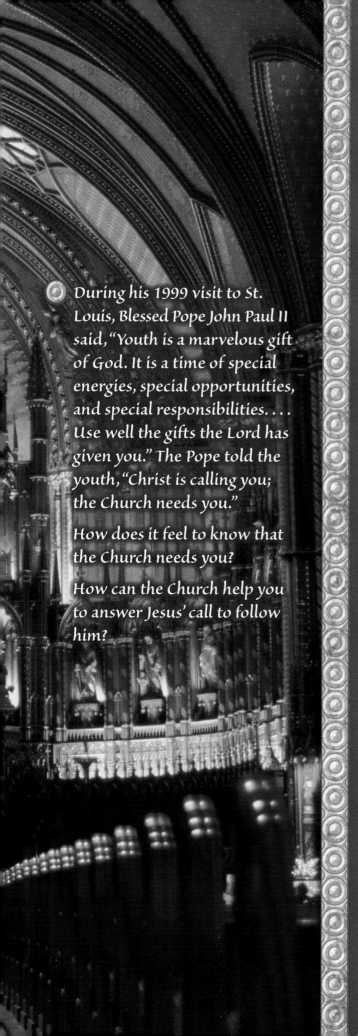

During his 1999 visit to St. Louis, Blessed Pope John Paul II said, "Youth is a marvelous gift of God. It is a time of special energies, special opportunities, and special responsibilities.... Use well the gifts the Lord has given you." The Pope told the youth, "Christ is calling you; the Church needs you."

How does it feel to know that the Church needs you?

How can the Church help you to answer Jesus' call to follow him?

① Jesus invites us to follow him in his Church.

From the very beginning of his public ministry, Jesus called people to follow him. People listened to his message about God the Father and the coming of his Kingdom. They heard his promise of new life.

More and more people responded to Jesus' invitation to follow him. Among his followers, the Apostles were a special group handpicked by Jesus. They stayed with Jesus and traveled together. They got to know Jesus and one another. The Apostles shared in Jesus' mission and authority, and Jesus gave them the power to continue his preaching and healing. With them Jesus formed the community we call the Church.

The **Church** is the community of people who believe in Jesus Christ, have been baptized in him, and follow his teachings. Members of the Church are called Catholics. The Catholic Church is rooted in beliefs, sacraments, and ministry that go back through the centuries to Jesus and the Apostles.

Jesus Christ, the Son of God, is the cornerstone of the Church and the source of our identity as its members. But God the Holy Spirit is our unending life force:

- making us one, preserving the Church in its true identity as the faith community founded by Christ
- calling us to worship and pray
- leading the Church in teaching, serving, and governing.

At the Sunday celebration of the Eucharist we pray this ancient profession of faith: "We believe in one holy catholic and apostolic Church." This is our belief, and it is a good description of the Church.

One, holy, catholic, and apostolic—these are the four identifying **Marks of the Church**, or essential characteristics of the Church begun by Jesus Christ. Through these characteristics the Church is known and recognized. But we, the members of the Church, could not bring about these characteristics alone. It is by Christ and through the Holy Spirit that the Church is one, holy, catholic, and apostolic.

> Describe the Church. What role does the Holy Spirit play in the life of the Church?

 The Church is one and holy.

At the Last Supper Jesus prayed to his Father for his followers "that they may be one just as we are" (John 17:11). In the first letter to the Corinthians, Saint Paul also spoke of the Christian community as one. He spoke of the Church in terms of the body. The body has a marvelous unity. Each part has its own function, and all parts work for the good of the whole body.

Saint Paul wrote, "Now you are Christ's body, and individually parts of it" (1 Corinthians 12:27). Being *one*, then, is a Mark of the Church. She is one, brought into unity by the unity of the Father, Son, and Holy Spirit. Her members together form the one Body of Christ, with Jesus Christ as the head, and with the Holy Spirit as the source of its life, unity, and gifts.

In his letter to the Ephesians, Saint Paul identified some of the things that make us one. This is how he encouraged his fellow Christians to live as one:

> I . . . urge you to live in a manner worthy of the call you have received, with all humility and gentleness, with patience, bearing with one another through love, striving to preserve the unity of the spirit through the bond of peace: one body and one Spirit, as you were also called to the one hope of your call; one Lord, one faith, one baptism; one God and Father of all, who is over all and through all and in all. Ephesians 4:1–6

As Catholics we celebrate our unity in the Eucharist. As a community we are nourished by the Sacrament of the Eucharist, the Body and Blood of Christ, and are strengthened in our one common faith. We also celebrate the other sacraments and have as our leaders the bishops.

Do YOU Know?

The pope and the bishops sometimes come together to discuss and make decisions on issues of faith, morals, and the life of the Church. These gatherings are called **Ecumenical Councils**. When Ecumenical Councils solemnly define a doctrine as being divinely revealed, they do so with the gift of infallibility. *Infallibility* is the Gift of the Holy Spirit that keeps the Church free from error —in her beliefs and teachings—in matters concerning Divine Revelation and the Deposit of Faith. The pope also has the gift when he specifically defines a doctrine pertaining to faith and morals.

Holiness is another mark by which we identify the Church. People are not born holy. Only God is holy. Our holiness is always a share in God's holiness. But by his Death and Resurrection, Jesus prepared the way for people to become holy. He calls us to be a holy people dedicated to God, the Holy One, and dedicated to one another.

In our lives, we are called to carry out our loving relationship with God and with one another. One way we do this is through prayer, especially the celebration of the sacraments, and by serving others.

Holiness describes those who listen to the Gospel message and respond to it. Our daily challenge is to live as Jesus taught. Only by trying consciously to do what is right can we begin to grow in holiness. Throughout the ages the Church has guided many people to lead holy lives. Holiness is an essential characteristic of the Church.

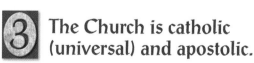

What are some signs that the Church is one? that the Church is holy?

3 The Church is catholic (universal) and apostolic.

Another identifying Mark of the Church is that it is *catholic*—universal and worldwide. This means that the Church welcomes everyone equally to hear and accept the Good News of Jesus' Salvation for all. The Church is everywhere, including people of every race, color, nationality, and economic status. The Church exists in all cultures and languages, celebrating the one mystery of Jesus Christ in diverse liturgical traditions, or rites.

People of God, like *Body of Christ*, is an image of the Church that we find in the New Testament. This image comes from Old Testament times. God chose the people of Israel to be his people. The early Christians saw themselves as part of the continuing story of God's people, growing into the Church of Christ. The People of God are spread throughout the world, and all enter into the People of God in the same way: by faith and Baptism.

Jesus entrusted his Church to his Apostles, his chosen leaders whom he had formed in faith. Jesus had confidence in his Apostles, and he assured them that the Holy Spirit would always be with them. The Holy Spirit would help them preach the Good News to the whole world. From its beginning, the Church has been missionary.

Jesus told his Apostles:

> All power in heaven and on earth has been given to me. Go, therefore, and make disciples of all nations . . . teaching them to observe all that I have commanded you. And behold, I am with you always, until the end of the age.
> Matthew 28:18–20

With the coming of the Holy Spirit on Pentecost, the Church became the visible sign of Christ's continuing work in the world. Jesus had handed over the roles of leadership and service in his community to Peter and the other Apostles. As the Church grew, it was built on the faith of the Apostles. This is why we say the Church is *apostolic*, another identifying Mark of the Church.

The Apostles' authority and call to service have been handed down to their

successors, the pope and bishops of the Catholic Church. This is what we call **apostolic succession**. The pope, the bishop of Rome, is the successor to Saint Peter. The pope leads the whole Church with his brother bishops. The pope and bishops are the authentic teachers of the Church. They teach the People of God the faith which is to be believed and applied in moral life. The Church continues to be taught, sanctified (made more holy), and guided by the pope and bishops.

There are other Christian communities in the world besides the Catholic Church. As Catholics we respect these communities and recognize Christ working in them. With them we pray that unity among all who believe in Jesus will be realized.

All Christian churches are not the same, however. The fullness of Christ's action and the working of the Holy Spirit are realized in the Catholic Church. All Salvation comes from Christ, the head through the Church, his Body. And to every generation the Church shares all that she believes through her teaching, worship, and her life.

How do the pope and bishops continue the work of the Apostles?

GROWING IN FAITH

PRAY

✝ We are called, we are chosen.
We are Christ for one another.
We are promised to tomorrow,
while we are for him today.
We are sign, we are wonder.
We are sower, we are seed.
We are harvest, we are hungry.
We are question, we are creed.
"Anthem"
Tom Conry

REFLECT & ACT

We all share in the mission to bring Christ to all people. We are called to share who Christ is and why he is so important.

What actions can you take in your neighborhood or school to share what you know and how you feel about Jesus?

REMEMBER
The Church teaches...

◎ The Church is the community of people who believe in Jesus Christ, have been baptized in him, and follow his teachings.

◎ The Church has four identifying marks: The Church is one, holy, catholic, and apostolic. By these four essential characteristics Jesus' Church is known and recognized.

◎ The Holy Spirit guides and preserves the Church in its true identity as the faith community founded by Christ.

◎ Christ is the cornerstone of the Church. All Salvation comes from Christ through the Church.

◎ Peter and the Apostles were the first leaders of the Church. The apostolic authority and call to service are handed down to their successors: the pope and bishops who teach, sanctify, and govern the Catholic Church.

Faith Words

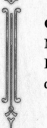

Church (p. 43)
Marks of the Church (p. 44)
Ecumenical Councils (p. 44)
apostolic succession (p. 46)

How is your life different from the lives of those who are not Catholic?

The Seven Sacraments

Wondrous truths, and manifold as wondrous,
  God hath written in these stars above;
But not less in the bright flowerets under us
  Stands the revelation of his love.

Bright and glorious is that revelation,
  Written all over this great world of ours;
Making evident our own creation,
  In these stars of earth, these golden flowers.

"Flowers"
Henry Wadsworth Longfellow

 # God uses signs to show us his love and power.

A sign is something visible that tells us about something that is often invisible. From the pages of the Old Testament we learn that God's chosen people lived by signs. These signs showed that God was acting among his people and shaping their lives. People interpreted even the ordinary things that happened as signs of God's action in their lives. The rain, the light and warmth of the sun, a growing family, a long life, and a homeland all signified God's care.

God met both the physical and spiritual needs of his people. He knew that the Israelites were suffering greatly while they were enslaved in Egypt. God called Moses to lead the Israelites out of Egypt and slavery. As they wandered in the desert in search of a place to live, God protected them. When they cried for water and food, God made water flow from a rock and sent them *manna*, "bread from heaven." These were signs to the chosen people that they could always depend on God because he was always with them.

An event, a community tradition, or a person can be a sign. God sent prophets to the Israelites to speak for him and to remind the people of his love. We read in the Old Testament about such prophets as Isaiah, Ezekiel, and Jeremiah—men who sometimes scolded the people, calling them to change their ways. These prophets were signs of God's concern for the people.

Jesus Christ himself is the greatest gift of the Father's love. In his interactions with people, Jesus always showed God's love. Like a parent bending to comfort or feed a child or to soothe a family's fears, Jesus was there caring for people in need. In his life and his teaching, Jesus made it clear to us that he was concerned about the needs of everyone.

- Jesus fed the hungry, taught the ignorant, and brought people back to God's love and friendship.

- Jesus met the blind, the deaf, the lame, and the sick—and healed them. He showed them God's power and mercy, and saved them.

These works showed Jesus' compassion, but they also showed more. By his words and his actions, Jesus showed that he was divine. Jesus Christ is the Son of God, the second Person of the Blessed Trinity who became man. In him we see, hear, and touch God. He is the greatest gift of God's love because he is God.

The Church is a sign and instrument of God's life and love among us.

After Pentecost the Apostles and first disciples set about the task of spreading the Good News of Jesus Christ. Since that time, men and women of faith have sought to establish the Church in every nation throughout the world.

By proclaiming and living out the Gospel message, the Church continues what Jesus began. In the community of the Church, we meet the Blessed Trinity. We meet Father, Son, and Spirit when we pray and worship together, and when we follow Jesus' way of living.

It is in the Church that God shares his grace, or life and friendship, with us. The Church, therefore, is an instrument of God's grace. Through the Church we can be united

Why do we say that Jesus is the greatest gift of God's love? How did he show God's love and power?

with God. The Church is also a sign of God's grace among us. Through the Church we can be united with one another. We are united in carrying out Jesus' mission of service to others. The Church helps us to help others and to live as Jesus did.

Among the ways that the Church is a sign of God's grace are particular acts of worship, or community celebrations, that we call sacraments. Sacraments are events that are signs, too. **Sacraments** are effective signs given to us by Jesus Christ through which we share in God's life. God acts through the sacraments to effect, or cause to happen, the very thing for which these signs stand.

By the power of the Holy Spirit, Jesus is present in the Church in a unique way in his sacraments. The sacraments help us to grow in holiness, to build up the Body of Christ, and to give worship and praise to God.

Describe how the Church is a sign and an instrument of God's love in the world.

 Through the Seven Sacraments we share in God's grace.

There are Seven Sacraments, and in each one God invites us to share in his life in a special way. Each of the Seven Sacraments —Baptism, Confirmation, the Eucharist, Penance and Reconciliation, the Anointing of the Sick, Holy Orders, and Matrimony— marks a particular time in our growth as a Christian.

The Church invites us to full participation in Christ's life through the *Sacraments of Christian Initiation*: Baptism, Confirmation, and the Eucharist. Through these three sacraments we are welcomed into the Church, strengthened in faith by the Holy Spirit, and nourished by Christ himself.

- Baptism is the first sacrament of our initiation into the Church. To be baptized means to be born anew, to share in Christ's life. Through Baptism, we become children of God, are freed from sin, and are welcomed into the Church.

- In Confirmation, we receive the Gift of the Holy Spirit in a special way.

- Through the Eucharist we complete our initiation into the Church. The Eucharist is the Sacrament of Christ's Body and Blood. For the rest of our lives we will be nourished, and our life of grace will be sustained, when we receive Holy Communion.

Two other sacraments, Penance and the Anointing of the Sick, are known as *Sacraments of Healing*. Even though we begin a new life of grace through the Sacraments of Initiation, we are still subject to suffering, illness, and sin. These two Sacraments of Healing restore and strengthen our life of grace.

In the celebration of the Sacrament of Penance, also known as the Sacrament of Reconciliation, the Church experiences God's loving forgiveness. Those who are truly sorry for their sins and are firmly committed to sin no more, turn back to God. Their relationship with God and the Church is restored, and their sins are forgiven.

The Sacrament of the Anointing of the Sick calls upon the whole Church to care for its sick or aged members. In this sacrament God's grace and comfort are given to those who are seriously ill, or who are suffering because of their old age. Through this sacrament they are united to the suffering of Christ and receive God's grace.

Finally, the Church has two *Sacraments at the Service of Communion*: Holy Orders and Matrimony. These two sacraments are concerned with the Salvation of others. These sacraments give those who receive them a particular mission, or role, in the building up of the Church.

In the Sacrament of Holy Orders, baptized men are ordained to serve the Church as bishops, priests, and deacons.

What is a sacrament? Why are the sacraments important?

Bishops, priests, and deacons have different roles and responsibilities in their service to the community, but they all receive the Sacrament of Holy Orders. Only bishops, however, receive the fullness of Holy Orders.

In the Sacrament of Matrimony, a man and a woman become husband and wife and promise to be faithful to each other for the rest of their lives. The priest and community witness to their vows to love each other as Christ loves his Church. This sacrament perfects the love the spouses share and strengthens their unity. Through this sacrament the married couple help each other to live holy lives in service to each other and to the community. They welcome children into their lives and create a home of faith, prayer, and love.

The sacraments are truly sources of life for us. They nourish and strengthen our faith, and in them the faith-filled community of the Church meets the risen Christ.

Growing in Faith

PRAY

In the sacraments, we begin with signs we can see, feel, or hear: water, oil, bread and wine, human words and gestures. God acts through the ordinary to make our lives extraordinary. Blessing and praising God is one way we respond to God's action in our lives. Pray together the following psalm:

✝ Sing to the LORD a new song;
    sing to the LORD, all the earth.
Sing to the LORD, bless his name;
    announce his salvation day after day.
Tell God's glory among the nations;
    among all peoples, God's marvelous
    deeds.
Psalm 96:1–3

REMEMBER
The Church teaches...

- ◉ Jesus Christ is God's greatest gift. In Jesus we meet the invisible God in a visible way.

- ◉ The Church is the visible sign and instrument by which we meet God.

- ◉ The Seven Sacraments are effective signs given to us by Jesus Christ through which we share in God's life.

- ◉ The sacraments help us to grow in holiness, to build up the Body of Christ, and to give worship to God.

Faith Words

sacraments (p. 51)
parish (p. 52)
pastor (p. 52)
diocese (p. 52)

REFLECT & ACT

Have you ever seen God through the actions of someone else? Describe that person and tell how he or she acted.

What sacraments have you received? How can receiving those sacraments help you to bring Jesus' message to your neighborhood or community?

Becoming Catholic

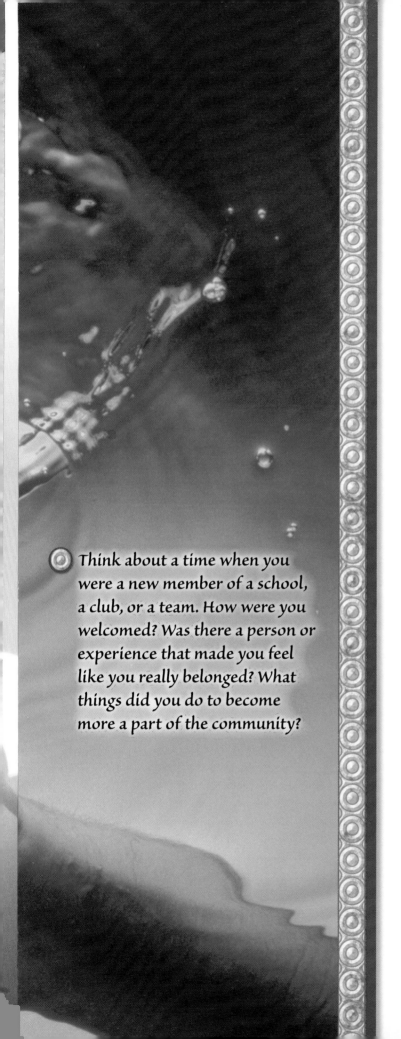

Think about a time when you were a new member of a school, a club, or a team. How were you welcomed? Was there a person or experience that made you feel like you really belonged? What things did you do to become more a part of the community?

 ## In the Sacrament of Baptism we are welcomed into the Church.

The Gospel of Matthew concludes with Jesus telling his first disciples, "Go, therefore, and make disciples of all nations, baptizing them in the name of the Father, and of the Son, and of the holy Spirit" (Matthew 28:19).

These words show us some very important things about the Church and about our life in the Church. They show us that the Church is universal—it is open to all people, everywhere, and all are invited to be one with Christ. These words show us that we begin our life in the Church through the Sacrament of Baptism; we share this sacrament with every member of the Church.

Each of us in the Church is welcomed in Baptism, and each of us is called to welcome others. In our world today people are too often left out, cut off, or held back. Some are even favored at the expense of others. The Church tries to welcome all without distinction. This, after all, is what Jesus did.

Some of the first words we hear from the priest or deacon at Baptism are words of welcome. These words are a part of our initiation into the Church. We call the process of becoming a member of the Church *Christian Initiation*. We are initiated into the Church through the Sacraments of Baptism, Confirmation, and Eucharist.

While our full initiation into the Church always consists of these three sacraments, the process of initiation can vary. Many people are baptized as infants. If we were baptized as babies, we were baptized in the faith of the Church. Our parents and godparents affirmed their own faith and promised to help us grow as faithful Christians.

A. Choose the correct term to complete each statement.

Confirmation	Pentecost	Gifts of the Holy Spirit
Apostles	Baptism	diocese
Christian Initiation	Holy Spirit	Holy
One	Apostolic	Catholic
Sacraments of Initiation	Infallibility	Church

1. The _____ is the third Person of the Blessed Trinity who guides and strengthens the Church.

2. A _____ is a local area of the Church led by a bishop.

3. The _____ is a name given to the Sacraments of Baptism, Confirmation, and Eucharist.

4. _____ is the day on which the Holy Spirit came to Jesus' first disciples as Jesus promised.

5. _____ is the Mark of the Church that describes the unity of the Church.

6. The _____ is the community of people who believe in Jesus Christ, have been baptized in him, and follow his teachings.

7. _____ is the first and foundational sacrament by which we become sharers in God's divine life, are freed from Original Sin and all personal sins, become children of God, and are welcomed into the Church.

8. _____ is the name given to the twelve men chosen by Jesus to share in his mission in a special way.

9. The Church is _____ because she shares in the holiness of God.

10. _____ is the process by which we become members of the Church.

11. _____ is the sacrament in which we receive the Gift of the Holy Spirit in a special way.

12. _____ means that the pope and bishops are guided in truth when defining the doctrines of faith and morals.

13. _____ is the Mark of the Church that identifies the Church as universal, open to all who believe.

14. The _____ help us to live as faithful followers and true witnesses of Jesus Christ.

15. _____ is the Mark of the Church that identifies the Church as founded by Christ on the Apostles.

B. Circle the response that does *not* belong.

1. Jesus told his followers that the Holy Spirit would
   a. remain with them forever.
   b. come to them on Good Friday.
   c. lead them to the truth.
   d. strengthen them to be his witnesses.

2. The Marks of the Church identify it as
   a. an exclusive closed community.
   b. a community dedicated to God and one another.
   c. based on apostolic authority.
   d. welcoming to all people.

3. The sacraments are
   a. life-giving signs of Christ's presence.
   b. acts of worship.
   c. seven in number.
   d. personal and private.

4. Through the Sacrament of Baptism we
   a. receive the Holy Spirit.
   b. are kept from sin forever.
   c. are reborn as children of God.
   d. become members of the Church.

5. Through the Sacrament of Confirmation we
   a. are anointed with holy oil.
   b. receive the Holy Spirit in a new way.
   c. have water poured on our head as a sign of cleansing.
   d. are strengthened with special Gifts of the Holy Spirit.

C. Share your faith by responding thoughtfully to these questions.

1. What signs do you see that show you God is truly present and active in our world today?

   _____

   _____

2. How is the Church a sign and an instrument of God's life and love among us?

   _____

   _____

3. Explain in your own words how Jesus acts in and through the sacraments.

   _____

   _____

4. What does it mean to you to be a witness to Christ? What would a person see or hear or sense in you that would show that you are a Catholic?

   _____

   _____

5. Reflect for a moment on a problem or decision you and other young people must face or make in today's world. How can your faith help you to make right choices?

   _____

   _____

A. Choose the correct term to complete each statement.

| sacraments | Divine Inspiration | Divine Revelation | Bible | Apostles |
| Grace | Gospels | Church | Paschal Mystery | Messiah |

1. The _____ is the community of people who believe in Jesus Christ, have been baptized in him, and follow his teachings.

2. The _____ are the twelve men chosen by Jesus to share in his mission in a special way.

3. _____ means "God's Anointed One," the Savior.

4. The accounts found in the New Testament of God's Revelation through Jesus Christ are known as the _____.

5. _____ is God making himself known to us.

6. _____ is the special guidance that the Holy Spirit gave to the human authors of the Bible.

7. The _____ is the written account of God's Revelation and his relationship with his people.

8. The _____ refers to the suffering, Death, Resurrection, and Ascension of Jesus Christ.

9. _____ is a participation, or sharing, in God's life and friendship.

10. _____ are effective signs given to us by Jesus Christ through which we share in God's life.

B. Describe in your own words these mysteries and beliefs of the Catholic Church.

1. The Incarnation: _____

   _____

2. The Blessed Trinity: _____

   _____

3. The Annunciation: _____

   _____

4. Pentecost: _____

   _____

5. Easter: _____

   _____

C. Circle the letter beside the correct response.

1. We become members of the Church through the Sacrament of
   a. Holy Orders.
   b. Grace.
   c. Baptism.
   d. Eucharist.

2. The part of the Bible in which we read about God and the early Israelites is the
   a. Old Testament.
   b. New Testament.
   c. Gospels.
   d. Revelation.

3. Faith is
   a. just another way of looking at life.
   b. a belief in things unseen.
   c. one of the sacraments.
   d. a feast of the Church.

4. Because we are made in God's image
   a. we are the same as all of his creatures.
   b. we have no soul.
   c. we can know and love God.
   d. we are not free to make choices.

5. By his actions, Jesus showed that he is
   a. only divine.
   b. only human.
   c. fully divine and fully human.
   d. half human and half divine.

D. Answer as completely and thoughtfully as you can.

1. What do we learn from the New Testament about Jesus Christ being truly human? about Jesus Christ being truly God's Son?

   _____

   _____

   _____

   _____

2. What are some images that Jesus used to describe the Kingdom of God? _____

   _____

   _____

3. How do the sacraments helps us to grow in faith and become stronger witnesses to Jesus Christ?

   _____

   _____

4. What does the story of Jesus' Resurrection mean to you? What hope does it give you?

   _____

   _____

5. How did the Holy Spirit help the first followers of Jesus? How is the Holy Spirit helping you?

   _____

   _____

The Eucharist

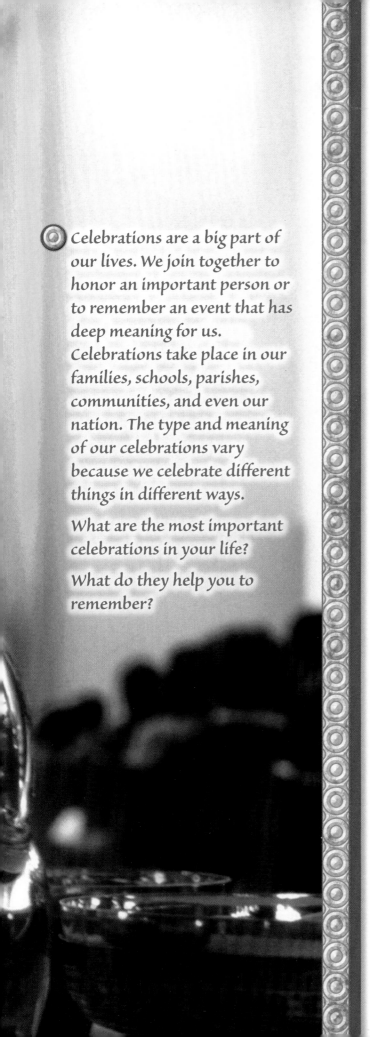

Celebrations are a big part of our lives. We join together to honor an important person or to remember an event that has deep meaning for us. Celebrations take place in our families, schools, parishes, communities, and even our nation. The type and meaning of our celebrations vary because we celebrate different things in different ways.

What are the most important celebrations in your life?

What do they help you to remember?

 Jesus gave us the Eucharist at the Last Supper.

In the Bible we read of many celebrations among the Israelites. Sacrifice was one of their chief forms of celebrating and worshiping the one true God. At their celebrations the Israelites remembered their past great moments of victory and deliverance. One celebration was more important to them than all others. In this celebration they remembered that God had freed them from slavery in Egypt by helping them to escape from their Egyptian masters.

On the night before this escape, the Israelites would save their newborn children from death if they did as their leader, Moses, told them. Speaking in God's name Moses ordered each Israelite family to kill a young lamb and to sprinkle its blood on the doorposts and frames of their homes. The people were then to have a special meal of roasted lamb, unleavened bread, wine, and bitter herbs:

> This is how you are to eat it: with your loins girt, sandals on your feet and your staff in hand, you shall eat like those who are in flight. It is the Passover of the LORD. For on this same night I will go through Egypt, striking down every first-born of the land. . . . But the blood will mark the houses where you are. Seeing the blood, I will pass over you.
> Exodus 12:11–13

This great event is known as the **Passover**, the feast on which Jewish people remember the miraculous way that God saved them from death and slavery in ancient Egypt. God also instructed Moses to tell the people to remember and celebrate this saving event always:

The Last Supper, Andy Warhol, 1986

This day shall be a memorial feast for you, which all your generations shall celebrate with pilgrimage to the LORD, as a perpetual institution. . . . Keep, then, this custom of the unleavened bread. Since it was on this very day that I brought your ranks out of the land of Egypt. . . .
Exodus 12:14,17

Centuries later Jesus celebrated this same Passover meal every year with his family and friends. On the night before he died, Jesus shared the Passover meal with his Apostles. At that meal, which Christians now call the Last Supper, Jesus explained that his life would be sacrificed.

- Through the shedding of his blood, the community of believers would be saved from sin and death.

- Through Jesus there would be a new and everlasting covenant with God.

Jesus' Last Supper was something very different from all other Passover meals that had been celebrated. This is the way part of it is described in Luke's Gospel:

Then he took the bread, said the blessing, broke it, and gave it to them, saying, "This is my body, which will be given for you; do this in memory of me." And likewise the cup after they had eaten, saying, "This cup is the new covenant in my blood, which will be shed for you."
Luke 22:19–20

The bread and wine still looked and tasted like bread and wine, but they were now what Jesus said they were: his very Body and Blood. Jesus told his Apostles to repeat in his memory what he had done at the Last Supper. They would do this in the **Eucharist**, the Sacrament of his Body and Blood. Through this sacred meal, they would remember what Jesus did for all of us by his Death and Resurrection. Jesus would be really present to them.

> Why were Jesus and his Apostles gathered at the Last Supper? What happened at the Last Supper?

Sunday, the "Lord's Day," is the principal day for celebrating the Eucharist because it is the day of the Lord's Resurrection. That is why we are obliged as faithful believers to participate in the Mass every Sunday or in the vigil Mass on Saturday evening. We are also obligated to participate in the Mass on Holy Days of Obligation.

> Why is the Sunday celebration of the Mass the most important action of our week?

 ## We celebrate the Eucharist at Mass.

Very shortly after Jesus' Resurrection the small community of believers began to do what Jesus had told them to do in his memory. They worshiped together as one people drawn together by the Holy Spirit and united in the risen Christ. Their celebrations consisted of listening to the Scriptures, reflecting on them, and recognizing Jesus' presence in the Eucharist.

Through history the celebration of the Eucharist has been called by many different names. Some of them are "the Lord's Supper," "the breaking of the bread," "the Holy Sacrifice," and the name *Eucharist* itself, which means, "to give thanks to God." However, the name most often used for the celebration of the Eucharist is **Mass**, the Church's great prayer of praise and thanks to God the Father.

When we gather to celebrate the Eucharist, the Holy Spirit is present. When we take part in our parish's weekly celebration of the Mass, we recall the great deeds of Jesus Christ by which he saved us. We thank God the Father for the gift of his Son, and through the power of the Holy Spirit the saving power of Jesus is made present to us. When we receive Holy Communion we share in God's life and are nourished and strengthened. We commit to living as God calls us to live.

Do YOU Know?

Our ancestors in faith used the term *covenant* to describe God's relationship with them. In the Bible a covenant is a solemn agreement between God and his people, frequently confirmed by a sacrifice to God or a solemn ritual. We read in the Old Testament that God made a covenant with Noah and all living beings after the flood. God made a covenant with Abraham and his descendants. God made a covenant with Moses on Mount Sinai. Jews today honor this covenant, keeping God's laws and following rituals established centuries ago.

In Jesus Christ God has established his new and everlasting covenant. Jesus' Death on the cross is the sacrifice of the new covenant—his life and Death restore humanity's relationship with God.

- asking God for mercy
- joining the priest in praying the Glory to God.

During the Liturgy of the Word we hear God's Word proclaimed to us. In each of the readings, we open our hearts and listen as a community to God as he speaks to us and guides us. The book containing all the readings that we use at Mass is called the **Lectionary**. It is not the whole Bible but a collection of parts of the Bible arranged for reading at Mass. The Church has chosen the Bible readings for each Mass to help us celebrate each Sunday and season. The Lectionary also has different readings for Masses during the week.

On Sundays there are usually three readings:

- The first reading is most often taken from the Old Testament. It recalls God's saving actions throughout history. We respond by saying or singing an Old Testament psalm.

- The second reading is taken from the New Testament, often from one of the letters, or Epistles, of Saint Paul. It is never taken from one of the Gospels.

- The third reading is always from one of the four Gospels (Matthew, Mark, Luke, or John). The reading of the Gospel is special. Only a deacon or priest can proclaim the Gospel, and everyone stands for its reading.

After the readings the priest or deacon gives a homily—or explanation of the readings—to help us better understand God's Word and how to live it. We respond to what we have heard in the readings and the homily by saying the Creed together. Then in the general intercessions, or prayer of the faithful, the needs of the Church, of the world, of those who suffer and are in need, and of the local community are remembered and offered to God.

 In the Liturgy of the Eucharist we offer and receive the gift of Jesus.

The second principal part of the Mass is the Liturgy of the Eucharist. It begins with the presentation and preparation of the gifts of bread and wine. These are the same simple, basic elements of human nourishment that Jesus used at the Last Supper. Members of the assembly present the gifts of bread and wine to the priest or deacon. He accepts these gifts as well as money or other gifts

What do we hear in the Liturgy of the Word? How do we respond to what we hear?

offered for the Church and the poor. The priest then prepares the bread and wine at the altar. These offerings will become for us the Body and Blood of Christ.

The **Eucharistic Prayer** is the heart of the celebration of the Mass. In this prayer the priest leads us in lifting up our hearts in praise and thanksgiving to God through Jesus Christ. All gathered give thanks to God the Father for his blessings.

The priest does and says what Jesus did and said at the Last Supper—what Jesus commanded us to do in memory of him. The priest says over the bread, "FOR THIS IS MY BODY," and over the wine, "FOR THIS IS THE CHALICE OF MY BLOOD." This is called the *Consecration*. Through the actions and words of the priest and by the power of the Holy Spirit, the bread and wine are changed and become the Body and Blood of Christ. The true presence of Jesus Christ in the Eucharist under the appearances of bread and wine is called the **Real Presence**.

The Church, gathered together in the unity of the Holy Spirit and united with Christ, offers the sacrifice of the Mass to God the Father. At Mass we also offer our own lives—our worries and needs as well as our joys—and join them to Christ's self-offering. After praying for our needs and for the members of the Church, both living and dead, we raise our voices in joyful praise and sing "Amen." With this response the Eucharistic Prayer ends.

The Lord's Prayer and the Sign of Peace move us toward receiving Holy Communion. Again following what Jesus himself did, the priest breaks the consecrated Host. Everyone sings or prays the Lamb of God. Those properly prepared receive the Body and Blood of Christ.

The Church teaches that to receive Holy Communion we must be free of serious sin. A person is freed from serious sin by celebrating the Sacrament of Penance and Reconciliation. As a sign of respect and reverence for the Eucharist, we must also have not taken any food or drink for one hour before receiving Holy Communion. This is called the **eucharistic fast**. Water and medicine may be taken during the eucharistic fast.

The Host may be received in the hand or on the tongue. If we receive the Host in the hand, we place it reverently in our mouths ourselves. All join in singing the Communion song, another sign of the unity of those gathered.

The Church encourages us to receive Holy Communion each time we participate in Mass. By receiving Holy Communion we are:

- nourished with the Sacrament of the Eucharist
- forgiven of our venial sins and strengthened to avoid serious sin
- made one with Christ and one another. We are no longer many. We are now one in the love of Christ.

> What gift do we offer to God at Mass? What gift does God offer us?

73

At the end of Mass we are sent forth to bring God's love to others.

Mass is a word taken from the Latin word for "sending forth." At the end of Mass the priest or deacon blesses the assembly and says, "Go in peace." This is the peace that Jesus promised to his friends. It is the peace that the world cannot give: the peace of Christ.

There are many ways we can bring the love of Christ to others:

- We can share our time and talents with others, realizing as we do that God acts in and through them. Others can experience God's love in and through us, by our faith and generosity.

- We can avoid all forms of injustice and prejudice based on race, sex, or nationality. In this way we can bring the peace of Christ to others.

- We can respect our bodies and the bodies of others as Temples of the Holy Spirit. In this we are living as Christ calls us.

By striving daily to grow closer to God and to all of God's people, we are living the Mass.

We should also remember that we are followers of Jesus Christ, who came, not to be served, but to serve. Ways we might serve the Lord include the following:

- caring for the poor, the sick, and the lonely

- respecting life, especially the dignity of human life

- participating in family, parish, and community activities.

Love

How does your participation in the Mass strengthen you to serve others?

Do YOU Know?

The liturgy is the work of the Body of Christ. As members of the Body of Christ, the Church, we are called to active participation at Mass through prayers, songs, gestures, actions, and silence. Just as each part of the Mass has a specific function, each of us gathered—the assembly, priest, deacon, altar servers, readers, extraordinary ministers of Holy Communion, and choir—has a specific role. Each person at Mass has an important role, and each of us helps everyone gathered to participate more fully in the Mass.

 Sin harms our relationship with God.

We know from the Old Testament that God is "a merciful and gracious God, slow to anger and rich in kindness and fidelity, continuing his kindness for a thousand generations, and forgiving wickedness and crime and sin" (Exodus 34:6–7). The greatest Teacher of God's mercy and compassion is Jesus, the Son of God. By the things he did and the way he lived, Jesus showed us God's mercy.

We all need God's forgiveness because we all are inclined to sin. When we freely choose to turn away from God and turn toward something that is not God, we sin. **Sin** is a thought, word, deed, or omission against God's law that harms us and our relationship with God and others. When we sin, our relationship with God is weakened by our unwillingness to live as God calls us to live.

Sin is always a personal choice. The world is a challenging place in which to live, and we are often tempted to do what is wrong. But a temptation is not a sin. It is an attraction to sin. Everyone is tempted. Even Jesus was tempted. In order to overcome temptation and avoid sin, we need God's grace to be strong in making good choices.

There are different types of sin. A **mortal sin** is a very serious sin that turns us completely away from God because it is a choice we freely make to do something that we know is seriously wrong. In order for a sin to be a mortal sin, three conditions are necessary:

- The sinful action or attitude must involve a grave and serious matter.

- We must have clear knowledge that what we are doing is mortally sinful.

- We must freely choose and fully consent to this serious evil.

77

All three conditions must be met for any sin to be considered mortal.

Less serious sin that weakens our friendship with God but does not turn us completely away from him is called **venial sin**. Venial sins do harm to others, to ourselves, or to our relationship with God and others.

Jesus taught us that God's mercy far exceeds any wrong or harmful action on our part. By his Death on the cross and his rising to new life, Jesus saves us from sin. We must be willing to admit our weakness, however, and to turn to God for forgiveness and compassion.

> What is sin? How does it affect our relationship with God and with others?

 We celebrate God's love and forgiveness.

Jesus Christ, the Son of God, forgave the sins of those who truly believed in him. Jesus willed that his Apostles do the same:

> "Peace be with you. As the Father has sent me, so I send you." And when he had said this, he breathed on them and said to them, "Receive the holy Spirit. Whose sins you forgive are forgiven them, and whose sins you retain are retained."
> John 20:21–23

Only bishops (the successors of the Apostles) and priests forgive our sins in the Sacrament of Penance and Reconciliation. They do this in the person of Christ and through the power of the Holy Spirit. The **Sacrament of Penance and Reconciliation** is the sacrament by which our relationship with God and the Church is restored and our sins are forgiven. We celebrate God's love and forgiveness.

When we are baptized, Original Sin and all the sins we have committed are forgiven. We are born into new life with Christ. The grace we receive at Baptism, however, does not keep us from sinning. We are still free to choose and to act, and at times we act without thinking of the consequences. But our conscience helps us to think about the consequences of our actions, and helps us to think before we act.

Conscience is our ability to know the difference between good and evil, right and wrong. Conscience is always to be formed by the teachings of Christ and his Church. We are called upon to continue forming our conscience throughout life and to obey the judgment of our conscience. Our conscience however, must be well-formed or we risk making wrong choices.

Our conscience is formed in many ways:

- by learning all we can about our faith and the teachings of the Church
- by praying to God, asking the Holy Spirit to strengthen and guide us
- by reading and reflecting on Scripture
- by seeking advice from wise people we respect, such as parents, teachers, parish priests, and responsible friends
- by examining our conscience on a regular basis, thinking about how we have treated God, ourselves, and others.

Sometimes we may not take the time to see the impact our choices and actions have. We lose sight of where we are going. We may not realize the positive direction our lives have taken, or that we have strayed from the path that God calls us to take. When we examine our conscience, we honestly ask ourselves about our relationship with God and others.

When we receive the Sacrament of Penance we must confess our serious sins and should even confess our less serious sins.

Have you ever had a disagreement with someone and then reconciled with the person? Think about what happened. What did you do? What did the other person do?

Do YOU Know?

During an examination of conscience, we ask the Holy Spirit to help us judge the direction of our lives. Here are some possible questions you can ask yourself:

- Do I make anyone or anything more important to me than God? Have I found time to read Scripture and listen to God's word? Do I pray?
- Have I treated God's name and the name of Jesus with reverence?
- Do I participate in Mass and keep Sunday holy by what I say and do?
- Have I respected, obeyed, and cared for my parent(s) and guardians? Have I been kind and considerate to my brothers and sisters?
- Am I a person who respects all life? Am I patient with the elderly, aware of the hungry and homeless, and respectful of those different from me?
- Do I treat my own body and the bodies of others respectfully? Have I harmed myself, or encouraged others to harm themselves, by improper use of things like drugs, alcohol, or food?
- Have I been selfish or stolen anything from anyone? Have I shared my belongings?
- Am I a truthful person? Have I been fair and honest with friends, family, teachers, and myself?
- Do I try to do God's will in my relationships with others? Have I been happy for others when they have the things they want or need?
- Have I made God my treasure rather than material possessions?

We celebrate the Sacrament of Penance.

As we prepare to seek and receive God's forgiveness, we should examine our conscience quietly and prayerfully. We should focus on whatever might separate us from God's life of grace. But we should also confess our venial sins as well. You may want to discuss this with the priest to whom you will confess your sins.

We can celebrate the Sacrament of Penance individually or communally. When we assemble as a community to celebrate the sacrament, each of us meets with the priest individually and privately for confession and absolution. There are four main parts to the Sacraments of Penance:

- *Contrition.* Contrition is sorrow for our sins with a firm purpose not to sin again. When our contrition comes from believing in God and loving him it is called perfect contrition. Contrition is the most important act of the penitent, or person seeking forgiveness and reconciliation. Sadness for the sin and the desire to sin no more must be genuine. Our intention must be to sin no more.

- *Confession of sins.* The penitent speaks with the priest, telling him what sins were committed. In confessing our sins we take responsibility for our actions and can be reconciled with God and the Church. The priest cannot tell anyone what he has heard in confession. We call this the seal of confession.

- *Penance.* Since sin weakens us and our relationship with God and others, we need to do something to show we are sorry for the sin. The priest gives us an act of penance to perform, such as saying a prayer or doing a good deed.

- *Absolution.* The priest, in the person of Christ and through the power of the Holy Spirit, absolves (forgives) the penitent's sins. The priest makes the Sign of the Cross over the penitent and says the prayer of absolution.

The Sacrament of Penance is a wonderful way to praise God and thank him for his mercy and forgiveness. It is also a way to grow in God's life of grace and in the love of one another.

The Church Celebrates the Sacrament of Penance

Rite for Reconciliation of Individual Penitents

The priest greets me.

I make the Sign of the Cross.
The priest asks me to trust in God's mercy.

He or I may read something from the Bible.

I talk with the priest about myself.
I confess my sins.
The priest talks to me about loving God and others.
He gives me a penance.

I make an Act of Contrition.
In the name of God and the Church, the priest gives me absolution. (He may extend or place his hands on my head.)

Together the priest and I give thanks to God for his forgiveness.

Rite for Reconciliation of Several Penitents with Individual Confession and Absolution

We sing an opening hymn and the priest greets us. The priest prays an opening prayer.

We listen to a reading from the Bible and a homily.

We examine our conscience.
We make an Act of Contrition.
We may say a prayer or sing a song, and then pray the Our Father.

Each of us then meets individually and privately with the priest.

I confess my sins. The priest gives me a penance.

In the name of God and the Church, the priest gives me absolution. (He may extend or place his hands on my head.)

After everyone has met with the priest, we join together to conclude the celebration. The priest blesses us, and we go in the peace and joy of Christ.

GROWING IN FAITH

PRAY

✝ Lord Jesus,
you chose to be called
the friend of sinners.
By your saving death and resurrection
free me from my sins.
May your peace take root in my heart
and bring forth a harvest
of love, holiness, and truth.
Amen.

REMEMBER
The Church teaches...

◎ Sin is freely choosing—by thought, word, deed, or omission—to do something that we know is wrong and against God's will.

◎ Our conscience is our ability to know the difference between good and evil, right and wrong.

◎ In the Sacrament of Penance, our sins are forgiven. We are reconciled to God, the Church, and one another.

◎ Priests act in the person of Christ to forgive our sins.

◎ The sins that we confess to the priest are protected by the seal of confession, which obliges the priest to total secrecy.

Faith Words

sin (p. 77)
mortal sin (p. 77)
venial sin (p. 78)
Sacrament of Penance
and Reconciliation (p. 78)
conscience (p. 78)

REFLECT & ACT

Is it difficult for you to ask forgiveness from God, the Church, or someone else? Why or why not?

Why do we call the sign of God's love and forgiveness the Sacrament of Penance?

A. Choose the correct term to complete each statement.

Venial sins	Holy Communion	Passover
Consecration	sin	Mass
Lectionary	conscience	Liturgy of the Word
Contrition	Sacrament of Penance and Reconciliation	liturgy
Liturgy of the Eucharist	Sunday	Eucharist

1. The _____ is the sacrament by which our relationship with God and the Church is restored and our sins are forgiven.

2. The _____ is the celebration of the Eucharist; the Church's great prayer of praise and thanks to God the Father.

3. _____ is the feast on which Jewish people remember the miraculous way that God saved them from death and slavery in ancient Egypt.

4. _____ is the Body and Blood of Christ that we receive and by which we are nourished in the Mass.

5. The _____ contains the collection of readings from the Bible that are proclaimed at Mass.

6. The _____ is part of the Mass during which we hear God's Word proclaimed.

7. Our _____ is our ability to know the difference between good and evil, right and wrong.

8. The _____ is the part of the Mass in which we offer and receive the gift of Jesus.

9. The _____ is the Sacrament of the Body and Blood of Christ.

10. The _____ is the part of the Eucharistic Prayer when the priest says and does what Jesus did at the Last Supper.

11. _____ is a thought, word, deed, or omission against God's law that harms us and our relationship with God and others.

12. _____, is the Lord's Day, the principal day for celebrating the Eucharist.

13. The _____ is the official public prayer of the Church.

14. _____ is sorrow for sins with a firm purpose not to sin again.

15. _____ are less serious sins that weaken our relationship with God but do not turn us completely away from him.

B. Circle the response that does *not* belong.

1. On the first Passover the Israelites
   a. refused to listen to Moses, their leader.
   b. killed a young lamb.
   c. sprinkled the lamb's blood on their doorposts.
   d. ate a special meal.

2. On the night before he died, Jesus
   a. celebrated Passover with his friends.
   b. explained to his disciples that his life would be sacrificed.
   c. was crucified.
   d. gave us the Eucharist.

3. When we celebrate Mass we
   a. share in Christ's Paschal Mystery.
   b. participate in a meal and a sacrifice.
   c. commit to living as God calls us to live.
   d. are freed from Original Sin.

4. In the Sacrament of Penance and Reconciliation
   a. our sins are forgiven.
   b. we are reconciled to God.
   c. we experience God's mercy.
   d. our intention is to sin again.

5. The Eucharist is
   a. our first welcoming into the Church.
   b. a meal because Jesus said, "Take and eat."
   c. a sacrifice because it is a memorial of Jesus' Death.
   d. the Church's great prayer of thanksgiving.

C. Share your faith by responding thoughtfully to these questions.

1. How did Jesus want his disciples to remember him? _____
   _____
   _____

2. What would help you understand and participate more fully in the Mass?
   _____
   _____
   _____

3. At the end of Mass we are "sent forth" to love and serve others. What does that mean to you?
   _____
   _____
   _____

4. What can you do to form your conscience so that you will make right choices? _____
   _____
   _____

5. How can celebrating the Sacrament of Penance help you to be more forgiving of others?
   _____
   _____
   _____

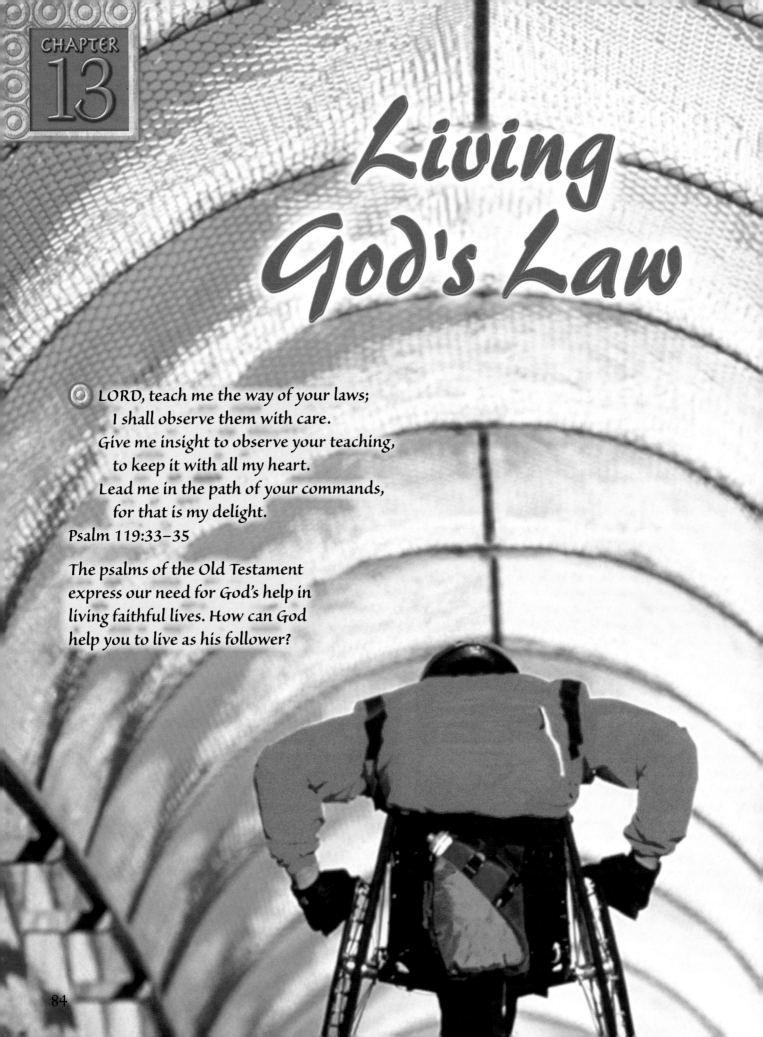

Living God's Law

◎ LORD, teach me the way of your laws;
    I shall observe them with care.
    Give me insight to observe your teaching,
        to keep it with all my heart.
    Lead me in the path of your commands,
        for that is my delight.

Psalm 119:33–35

The psalms of the Old Testament
express our need for God's help in
living faithful lives. How can God
help you to live as his follower?

 The Ten Commandments teach us how to live as God's people.

Over and over again God reached out with love to the Israelites. From the Old Testament we learn that God wanted to form them into a holy people, a nation that would be set apart. And God did this by entering into a covenant with them.

The Israelites cherished the covenant God made on Mount Sinai with their great leader Moses, who led them out of slavery in Egypt. The reason for this covenant was that God wanted the Israelites to be free, not only from physical and political bondage, but also from the spiritual slavery of sin.

God's covenant requires a response from the people. God revealed to Moses that the Israelites would have certain responsibilities in observing the covenant. We read in the Book of Exodus that "when Moses came to the people and related all the words and ordinances of the LORD, they all answered with one voice, 'We will do everything that the LORD has told us'" (Exodus 24:3). God's commands were summarized in what we now call the Ten Commandments. The **Ten Commandments** are the laws of God's covenant given to Moses on Mount Sinai.

The Catholic Church teaches that the Ten Commandments are God's law for us, too, and that no human law can change them. When we are faithful to God and obey his commandments, we grow closer to him in friendship and love. When we live by the Ten Commandments, we grow in holiness and happiness.

The first three commandments focus on our direct relationship with God. The remaining seven center on our relationship with ourselves and one another.

The First Commandment reminds us that we worship and serve the one true God. God alone is our Salvation. False gods, such as the exaggerated desire for power, wealth, or popularity, do not give us what God does. Denying God's existence, atheism, is a sin against the First Commandment.

When we live by the spirit of this commandment, we place our trust in the one true God, not in superstitious or occult practices. We adore God when we acknowledge that he is the Creator and Savior and that we are totally dependent upon him for our life and happiness. We pray and give witness to God and to our belief in him. The First Commandment calls us to believe in God, to hope in him, and to love him above all else.

The Second Commandment directs us to honor God's name. Respecting God's name is a sign of the respect that God, in all of his mystery and sacredness, deserves. The followers of Jesus show respect for his name and for the names of Mary and the saints. The Second Commandment also helps us to appreciate the gifts of speech and communication and to use them with care and respect.

Annual March for Life in Washington, D.C.

As Catholics we observe the Third Commandment by participating in the celebration of Mass on Sunday, the Lord's Day, and by keeping that day holy. We celebrate the Resurrection and the new life Christ has given us. The Church teaches that we are obligated to participate in Mass on Sundays and that we can keep Sunday holy in several ways:

- by participating in prayer
- by refraining from unnecessary work
- by serving the sick, elderly, and needy
- by spending time with our families.

Observing the Third Commandment helps us to develop family, social, and spiritual lives. We must be mindful of those who cannot rest on Sundays, and we should not place any unnecessary demands on others, so that they, too, can keep the Lord's Day.

THE TEN COMMANDMENTS

1. I am the LORD your God: you shall not have strange gods before me.
2. You shall not take the name of the LORD your God in vain.
3. Remember to keep holy the LORD's Day.
4. Honor your father and your mother.
5. You shall not kill.
6. You shall not commit adultery.
7. You shall not steal.
8. You shall not bear false witness against your neighbor.
9. You shall not covet your neighbor's wife.
10. You shall not covet your neighbor's goods.

How is our relationship with God strengthened by living out the first three commandments?

We are to respect human life and the human body by:

- avoiding anything that could injure or endanger life, such as uncontrolled anger, the use of narcotics, or excessive eating and drinking

- taking proper care of our own health

- caring for the environment in which all life flourishes.

The Sixth Commandment upholds the sacredness of the gift of the human person—body and soul—as made in the image and likeness of God. The gift of human sexuality helps us to express our partnership in God's created love. The Sacrament of Matrimony unites a man and woman in a sacred union. Anything or anyone who violates this vowed commitment through adultery, unfaithfulness, or abuse is harming God's gift of human sexuality. All sexual activity outside of marriage is wrong.

Every baptized person is called to the virtue of **chastity**, a gift from God that calls us to use our human sexuality in a responsible and faithful way. Our bodies are Temples of the Holy Spirit, and as such must be respected by ourselves and others. Our model of chastity is Jesus Christ.

The Sixth Commandment also reminds us to treasure our human sexuality, because it is something truly beautiful. Any action that violates or harms the dignity and sacredness of our bodies is wrong. Our understanding and appreciation of our human sexuality deepens as we learn to love and be loved by others.

② The Ten Commandments call us to live with respect for others.

The Fourth Commandment requires us that after honoring God, we should honor, respect, obey, and care for our parents and guardians. We should show honor, affection, and gratitude toward our extended families and the elderly. This respect also extends to all of those in authority, such as responsible government leaders, those in law enforcement, and teachers. In fulfilling the Fourth Commandment, we can imitate the way that Jesus showed love and respect toward Mary and Joseph.

The Fifth Commandment requires us to respect the sacredness of life and the dignity of the person. Murder, abortion, suicide, and euthanasia deny the gift of life. We believe that every human being—from conception to natural death—has the God-given right to life. Abortion is not a matter of choice.

In a world torn apart by violence, war, and ethnic and religious strife, the Church opposes armed conflict as a solution to political and social problems. In recent years the pope and the bishops of the United States have spoken out strongly against the use of nuclear and chemical weapons. God's law calls us to work untiringly for peace on earth.

Respect for the human person extends beyond direct killing of others or oneself.

> How can we live out the Fourth, Fifth, and Sixth Commandments?

3 The Ten Commandments call us to live responsibly.

The Seventh Commandment upholds justice in all its forms. This commandment protects the right of all people to share in God's gifts and to have equal respect. Stealing, cheating, and dishonesty in any form are against this commandment.

We are also reminded that jealousy and prejudice harm our relationship with God and others. Preoccupation with material goods will not bring the happiness that following God will. We are to use the resources we have to help poor and needy people. We should also use wisely and preserve the earth's resources.

Respect for truth is necessary in a society of openness and honesty. The Eighth Commandment holds us responsible for the truth. It teaches us to honor the good name of all people and to avoid anything that would injure another's reputation:

■ We are to tell the truth in all situations.

■ We are to respect the privacy of others, and keep a trust or confidence someone

has shared with us, unless someone will be harmed by our silence.

■ We are to treat all people with equal respect no matter their race, gender, religion, or age. This equality is the truth that comes from being made in God's image.

■ We are to give witness to the truth of Jesus Christ through our words and deeds.

The Ninth Commandment calls for a single-mindedness and control with regard to sexual matters. It calls us to a positive attitude toward our sexuality, which is only one dimension of our humanity. Purity of mind and heart requires modesty which is part of the virtue of temperance. **Modesty** is the virtue by which we dress, act, speak, and think in ways that show respect for ourselves and others. Pornography is visual violence. It harms the dignity and sacredness of our bodies.

The Tenth Commandment warns against envy, or any willful desire to possess property that belongs to others. Envy, which includes sadness at the sight of another's goods, has no place in our lives and cannot lead us to true happiness. This commandment also forbids greed and the desire to obtain earthly goods without limit. We are called to act and share with justice.

> How do the Ten Commandments keep us in a right relationship with God and others?

88

GROWING IN FAITH

PRAY

Living by the commandments gives us an inner peace and joy that no one can take away from us. But we need God's help in order to walk firmly in his way. And so we pray:

✝ Teach me, LORD, your way
that I may walk in your truth,
single-hearted and
revering your name.
Psalm 86:11

REFLECT & ACT

God gave us the Ten Commandments out of love. They are a clear path away from the unhappiness of sin to happiness with God.

Why do you think God's commandments direct us in the way to live and use our freedom?

REMEMBER
The Church teaches...

◎ The Ten Commandments guide us in our relationship with God and with one another. No human law can change them.

◎ The Ten Commandments are not mere rules; they are laws directing us to live the covenant we have with God.

◎ The first three commandments guide our relationship with God. The remaining seven commandments deal with our relationships to self and to others.

◎ Living according to the commandments is a serious responsibility. It is the only way to true happiness and peace.

Faith Words

Ten Commandments (p. 85)
chastity (p. 87)
modesty (p. 88)
virtue (p. 88)

What can you tell others about the commandments as a help to living a happier life?

Jesus' Way of Loving

Love is a word that we hear all the time and in many different situations. Some people say that the word has become overused and that the true meaning of love is lost.

What do you think the word love means?

How do your actions show love for your family and friends?

 Jesus asks us to love.

God's laws guided his people in the right way to live. At times, however, the people forgot or turned away from the way of God. In making the covenant and in giving the Ten Commandments, God wanted the people to observe the commandments out of love for him and for one another. The great prayer of the Old Testament summed up the commandments:

> Hear, O Israel! The LORD is our God, the LORD alone! Therefore, you shall love the LORD, your God, with all your heart, and with all your soul, and with all your strength.
> Deuteronomy 6:4–5

The people were also told, "You shall love your neighbor as yourself" (Leviticus 19:18). The Ten Commandments were concrete laws that showed them how to love God and neighbor.

Jesus observed and respected the laws of the covenant. He told his disciples, "Do not think that I have come to abolish the law or the prophets. I have come not to abolish but to fulfill" (Matthew 5:17).

Once a scholar asked Jesus which commandment in the law was the greatest. Jesus replied by bringing together the teachings of the Old Testament into the *Great Commandment*:

> You shall love the Lord, your God, with all your heart, with all your soul, and with all your mind. This is the greatest and the first commandment. The second is like it: You shall love your neighbor as yourself. The whole law and the prophets depend on these two commandments.
> Matthew 22:37–40

When the disciples of Jesus reflected on his life and teaching, they realized how important love was to Jesus. By word and example Jesus had urged them to love as he did.

He taught them to love God our Father totally. Everything that Jesus did was directed to his Father. We read that Jesus went off to the desert or to the mountains frequently to be alone with God and to pray. In fact, Jesus' whole life could be summed up as always doing the will of his Father.

So, it is not surprising that on the night before he died, Jesus told his disciples:

> I give you a new commandment: love one another. As I have loved you, so you also should love one another. This is how all will know that you are my disciples, if you have love for one another.
> John 13:34–35

This command from Jesus to his disciples is known as the **New Commandment**. Jesus wanted his disciples to love as he loved and to act as they knew he would act so that everyone they met would know him through them.

Later on, Jesus stressed that he himself had come as a perfect example of love for all of us. Jesus said to his disciples, "Love one another as I love you. No one has greater love than this, to lay down one's life for

> What can you do to love others as Jesus has loved you?

Do YOU Know?

The Blessed Virgin Mary is our most perfect model of faith, hope, and love. She entrusted herself entirely to God when she said, "May it be done to me according to your word" (Luke 1:38). Mary remained strong in hope despite the many difficulties and sorrows she faced as Jesus' mother. She expressed her deep faith in God in her Magnificat, or song. Throughout her life, Mary glorified God and loved Jesus and his disciples.

one's friends" (John 15:12–13). Jesus did lay down his life for us. And in doing so, Jesus showed how great his love for us was.

 2 The Beatitudes are guidelines for true happiness.

In the time of Jesus, God's people were again in need of someone to lead them to true freedom. As a nation they had suffered through many wars and domination by foreign rulers. They were looking for the Messiah to free them from this oppression and to show them the path to true freedom.

God had given the Israelites the gift of the Law of Moses as their way of life. Jesus wanted to teach again its lesson: love God and love neighbor. He told the people that his Father is the God of love, not of fear.

When Jesus spoke to the people, he sensed that their spirits were low. They had lost their way. Jesus challenged the people to take a giant step toward freedom, no matter how painful it seemed. Jesus promised that those who suffer for the sake of the Kingdom of God would be rewarded. In Matthew's Gospel, Jesus' Sermon on the Mount gives the way to true happiness called the Beatitudes.

The Beatitudes

Blessed are the poor in spirit,
  for theirs is the kingdom of heaven.

Blessed are they who mourn,
  for they will be comforted.

Blessed are the meek,
  for they will inherit the land.

Blessed are they who hunger and thirst
  for righteousness,
  for they will be satisfied.

Blessed are the merciful,
  for they will be shown mercy.

Blessed are the clean of heart,
  for they will see God.

Blessed are the peacemakers,
  for they will be called children of God.

Blessed are they who are persecuted for
    the sake of righteousness,
  for theirs is the kingdom of heaven.

Matthew 5:3–10

The **Beatitudes** are teachings that describe how to live as Jesus' disciples. They challenge us to live Jesus' way. Each one of them announces the spirit in which we are to live for God's Kingdom, or the *Kingdom of Heaven* as it is called in Matthew's Gospel. When we depend on God's love and not on possessions, when we show compassion, humility, and mercy, we are working to build up the Kingdom of God. This is also true when we choose to work for justice and peace despite challenges and difficulties.

In what ways can you live the spirit of the Beatitudes in your family, school, or neighborhood?

The Solitude of Christ, Maurice Denis, 1918

Jesus calls us to follow him in faith, hope, and love.

Christians of all times and places have tried to follow Jesus' New Commandment and live the Beatitudes. The early Christians discovered very quickly that to do this they would need a change of heart. They would have to live a life of virtue.

A virtue is a good habit that helps a person live according to God's love for us. Three virtues stand out as the most important of all: faith, hope, and charity. These are known as **theological virtues** because they have God as their source, motive, and object. They are gifts from God and mark the Christian way of life.

Faith is the gift from God by which we believe in God and all that he has revealed, and all that the Church proposes for our belief. Through the gift of faith we have a deep and abiding relationship with God, who loves us completely. Faith allows us to place our trust in God and to act as God wants us to. All disciples of Christ must not only keep the faith, but also profess it, witness to it by our words and actions, and pass it on to others.

Hope is the gift from God by which we desire eternal life, place our trust in Christ's promises, and rely on the help of the Holy Spirit. People of hope never give up on God, themselves, or on the relationship they have with God. They know that, even when things look bad, evil will not finally overcome good, and hatred will never extinguish love. This is the promise that Jesus made to us.

The challenge of hope is to act as God wants us to and to seek ways to work for justice and peace in the world. Hope helps us to remember that our true destiny is to be happy forever with God.

Saint Paul tells us that "faith, hope, love remain, these three; but the greatest of these is love" (1 Corinthians 13:13). The love we are speaking about, however, is the virtue of charity. **Charity** is the gift from God that enables us to love him above all things and to love our neighbor as ourselves.

With the help of this virtue, we follow the Great Commandment: We love God above all other things and our neighbors as ourselves. This love we have for God can become a powerful force in our lives and in our world. It can help us to appreciate our gifts and talents and to love ourselves as God loves us. It helps us to love even those who are known as our enemies.

To love others can be a joy, easy and immediately fulfilling. To love others can also require sacrifice, and the ability to forgive others and to welcome forgiveness in our own lives.

The gift of love is all around us. Jesus has shown us how to recognize it and how to use this gift in the world. This is the meaning of being a disciple of Christ.

> What or who helps you to be a loving, faithful, and hopeful person?

GROWING IN FAITH

PRAY

Silently reflect on these words of Saint Paul:

✝ Love is patient, love is kind. It is not jealous, [love] is not pompous, it is not inflated, it is not rude, it does not seek its own interests, it is not quick-tempered, it does not brood over injury, it does not rejoice over wrongdoing but rejoices with the truth. It bears all things, believes all things, hopes all things, endures all things. Love never fails.

1 Corinthians 13:4–8

REFLECT & ACT

Remember a happy time in your life. What brought you that happiness? How was it like or unlike the happiness of living the way Jesus wants us to?

REMEMBER
The Church teaches...

◎ Jesus taught the Great Commandment, to love God above all others and to love others as ourselves.

◎ Jesus offered us a New Commandment to love one another as Jesus has loved us.

◎ The Beatitudes are teachings that describe how to live as Jesus' disciples.

◎ Faith, hope, and charity are the theological virtues because they are gifts from God that have God as their source, motive, and object.

Faith Words

New Commandment (p. 92)
Beatitudes (p. 93)
theological virtues (p. 94)
faith (p. 94)
hope (p. 94)
charity (p. 94)

Saint Paul teaches us that love is much more than a feeling. What can you do to show love to the people in your life?

In the Service of Others

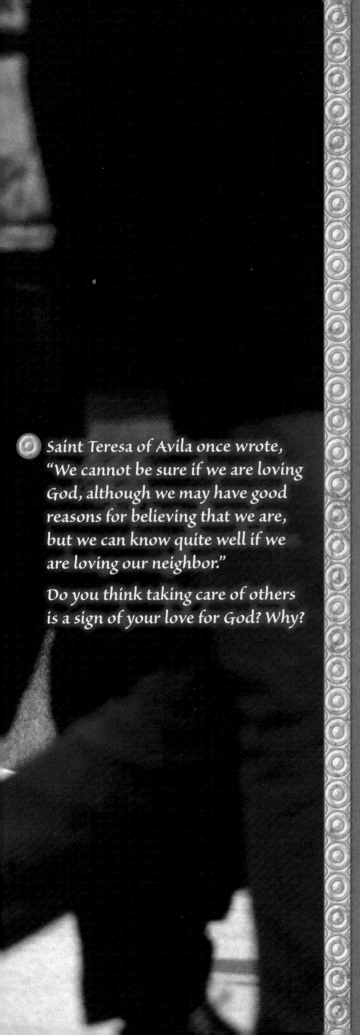

 ## We will be judged by our love.

Jesus' whole life was a shining example of service to others. He told his disciples, "I am among you as the one who serves" (Luke 22:27). When we help others, we are following in Jesus' footsteps.

When Jesus gave the Great Commandment to love God and our neighbors as ourselves, a scholar questioned him, asking, "And who is my neighbor?" (Luke 10:29) Jesus answered by telling the parable of the Good Samaritan.

According to the story a man who was on a journey was robbed, beaten, and left on the road to suffer. As he lay there, three people came along; but the first two passed by the suffering man. The third was a man from the country of Samaria, a hated enemy of the victim's country. The Samaritan stopped and took care of the man's wounds, brought him to an inn, and even paid for his care.

After telling the story Jesus asked who of the three men was a neighbor to the man attacked by robbers. The answer came, "The one who treated him with mercy"; and Jesus said, "Go and do likewise" (Luke 10:37).

At the end of our lives, how will we be judged for carrying out our Christian responsibilities? Jesus described the Last Judgment to help us understand the importance of our actions today. The **Last Judgment** is Jesus Christ's coming at the end of time to judge all people. We read in the New Testament that Jesus explained that some people will share in the joys of Heaven and the others will not. To those who performed deeds of mercy, Jesus will say:

> For I was hungry and you gave me food, I was thirsty and you gave me drink, a stranger and you welcomed me, naked and you clothed me, ill and you cared for me, in prison and you visited me.
> Matthew 25:35–36

Those being judged will ask him when they did all of these things for him, and Jesus will reply, "Amen, I say to you, whatever you did for one of these least brothers of mine, you did for me" (Matthew 25:40).

In his story of the Good Samaritan and his teaching on the Last Judgment, Jesus was talking about mercy. When we show mercy to someone who is suffering, we show love and compassion. Jesus taught that what we do for others, we are doing for him. The **Works of Mercy** are acts of love by which we care for the bodily and spiritual needs of others. They call us to live as Christ wants us to. The Works of Mercy are divided into two categories:

- The Corporal Works of Mercy focus on the physical and material needs of others.
- The Spiritual Works of Mercy focus on the needs of the heart, mind, and soul.

How could the world be different if we all lived out the Works of Mercy!

Do YOU Know?

Many parishes have programs to help their members practice the Works of Mercy. What programs in your parish can help you treat others as Jesus did?

Corporal Works of Mercy
Feed the hungry.
Give drink to the thirsty.
Clothe the naked.
Visit the imprisoned.
Shelter the homeless.
Visit the sick.
Bury the dead.

Spiritual Works of Mercy
Admonish the sinner.
Instruct the ignorant.
Counsel the doubtful.
Comfort the sorrowful.
Bear wrongs patiently.
Forgive all injuries.
Pray for the living and the dead.

 Catholic social teaching helps us to live Jesus' command to love others.

The Catholic Church teaches us that responding to the needs of others is a central part of our faith. **Catholic social teaching** is the teaching of the Church that calls all members to work for justice and peace as Jesus did. It commits us to the welfare of every person. It helps us see that each and every person shares the same human dignity. Catholic social teaching helps us follow Jesus' command to love others as he has loved us.

There are seven themes that are very important to the social teaching of the Church.

Life and Dignity of the Human Person
Human life is sacred because it is a gift from God. We are all God's children and share the

Students, teachers, and community members participate in a peace march and rally in Dorchester, Mass. on Sept. 11, 2006.

same human dignity from the moment of conception to natural death. Our dignity— our worth and value—comes from being made in the image and likeness of God. This dignity makes us equal. As Christians we respect all people, even those we do not know.

Call to Family, Community, and Participation

As Christians we are involved in our family life and community. We are called to promote the common good and to care for those most in need by participating in social, economic, and political life, using the values of our faith to shape our decisions and actions.

Rights and Responsibilities of the Human Person

Every person has a fundamental right to life. This includes the things we need to have a decent life: faith and family, work and education, health care and housing. We also have a responsibility to others and to society. We work to make sure the rights of all people are being protected.

Option for the Poor and Vulnerable

We have a special obligation to help those who are poor and in need. This includes those who cannot protect themselves because of their age or their health.

At different times in our lives we are all poor in some way and in need of assistance.

Dignity of Work and the Rights of Workers

Our work is a sign of our participation in God's work. People have the right to decent work, just wages, and safe working conditions, and to participate in decisions about their work. There is value in all work. Our work in school and at home is a way to participate in God's work of Creation. It is a way to use our talents and abilities to thank God for his gifts.

Solidarity of the Human Family

Solidarity affirms that we are all brothers and sisters, each responsible for the good of all. Each of us is a member of the one human family, equal by our common human dignity. The human family includes people of all racial, cultural, and religious backgrounds.

Name one way your parish can respond to Catholic social teaching, (see pages 98–100).

❖ Unit 4 Assessment ❖

A. Choose the correct term to complete each statement.

Beatitudes	Precepts of the Church	Ten Commandments
Resurrection	New Commandment	Corporal Works of Mercy
Communion of Saints	Virtue	Evangelization
Faith	Moses	Heaven
Hope	Charity	Spiritual Works of Mercy

1. The _____ are acts Christians are called to do to relieve the physical and material needs of others.

2. The _____ are laws of the Church that help us to see that loving God and others is connected to a life of prayer, worship, and service.

3. _____ means sharing the Good News of Jesus Christ and the love of God with all people, in every circumstance of life.

4. The _____ are teachings that describe how to live as Jesus' disciples.

5. _____ was the leader of the Israelites to whom God gave the Ten Commandments.

6. The _____ is the union of all the baptized members of the Church on earth, in Heaven, and in Purgatory.

7. The _____ are the laws of God's covenant given to Moses on Mount Sinai.

8. Christ's _____ gives us the hope of rising to new life after death.

9. The _____ calls us to love God and others as Jesus has loved us.

10. The _____ are acts Christians are called to do to relieve the spiritual, mental, and emotional needs of others.

11. A _____ is a good habit that helps us to act according to God's love for us.

12. _____ is the ultimate happiness of living with God forever.

13. _____ is the gift from God that enables us to love him above all things and our neighbor as ourselves.

14. _____ is the gift from God by which we desire eternal life, place our trust in Christ's promises, and rely on the help of the Holy Spirit.

15. _____ is the gift from God by which we believe in God and all that he has revealed, and all that the Church proposes for our belief.

B. Circle the response that does *not* belong.

1. God made a covenant with the Israelites so that they could
   a. have plenty to eat.
   b. be free from slavery in Egypt.
   c. be free from the slavery of sin.
   d. live as faithful people.

2. The theological virtues are
   a. hope.
   b. charity.
   c. courage.
   d. faith.

3. Catholic social teaching
   a. is founded on the life and work of Jesus.
   b. helps us to respect the dignity of all people.
   c. influences our work and our society.
   d. is a new teaching of the Church.

4. Jesus taught that at the end of life we will be judged on
   a. our power.
   b. our love.
   c. our service for others.
   d. our willingness to see him in others.

5. Catholics believe that when we die,
   a. life is changed, not ended.
   b. we live on only in our children.
   c. we are judged on how we loved God and others.
   d. death will be the beginning of endless happiness.

C. Share your faith by responding thoughtfully to these questions.

1. How do the Ten Commandments help us to be free?

   _____

   _____

2. Jesus' New Commandment might sound simple, but it demands strength and courage. Explain.

   _____

   _____

3. Recall the story of the Good Samaritan. What important lesson was Jesus teaching in this story?

   _____

   _____

4. Describe two Works of Mercy that you are able to perform in your life right now.

   _____

   _____

5. Why do you think Mary is considered the greatest saint?

   _____

   _____

A. Choose the correct term to complete each statement.

Eucharist	Human dignity	liturgy
Last Supper	Sacrament of Penance and Reconciliation	Mass
Sin	Conscience	Absolution
Venial sin	Confession	Immaculate Conception
Assumption	Real Presence	Church

1. The _____ is the truth that Mary was taken body and soul into Heaven.

2. The _____ is the community of people who believe in Jesus Christ, have been baptized in him, and follow his teachings.

3. The _____ was the Passover meal at which Jesus gave us the Eucharist.

4. _____ is our ability to know the difference between good and evil, right and wrong.

5. The _____ is the sacrament by which our relationship with God and the Church is restored and our sins are forgiven.

6. _____ is a thought, word, deed, or omission against God's law that harms us and our relationship with God and others.

7. _____ is the value and worth we share because God created us in his image and likeness.

8. _____ is a less serious sin that weakens our friendship with God but does not turn us completely away from him.

9. The _____ is the truth that God preserved Mary from Original Sin and all sin from the very moment she was conceived.

10. _____ is God's forgiveness of our sins through the words and actions of the priest in the Sacrament of Penance and Reconciliation.

11. The _____ is the Sacrament of the Body and Blood of Christ.

12. The _____ is the official public prayer of the Church.

13. _____ is the telling of one's sins to a priest in the Sacrament of Penance and Reconciliation.

14. The _____ is the celebration of the Eucharist.

15. The true presence of Jesus Christ in the Eucharist under the appearance of bread and wine is known as the _____.

B. Circle the letter beside the correct response.

1. The commandment that teaches us to respect the sacredness of life is
   a. the Eighth Commandment.
   b. the Fifth Commandment.
   c. the Fourth Commandment.
   d. the First Commandment.

2. The commandment that teaches us to respect the good name of others and to be honest is
   a. the First Commandment.
   b. the Ninth Commandment.
   c. the Sixth Commandment.
   d. the Eighth Commandment.

3. The commandment that teaches us to honor God's name and to show special reverence for the name of Jesus Christ is
   a. the Second Commandment.
   b. the Fourth Commandment.
   c. the Tenth Commandment.
   d. the Third Commandment.

4. "You shall confess your sins at least once a year" is one of the
   a. Ten Commandments.
   b. Beatitudes.
   c. Precepts of the Church.
   d. Marks of the Church.

5. The Church tells us that Mary
   a. was divine, not human.
   b. is the Mother of God and our mother, too.
   c. was kept by God from life's struggles.
   d. was not present at the Crucifixion.

C. Answer as completely and thoughtfully as you can.

1. As Christians we believe that we share in Christ's Resurrection. What does that mean to you?

_____

_____

2. As followers of Jesus Christ we are called to serve others in his name. How can someone your age do this? _____

_____

3. Mortal sin is the most serious sin against God. What three conditions make a sin mortal?

_____

_____

4. As Catholics we are to respond to the needs of others in our world. Tell about one of these needs that you would like to do something about, and why.

_____

_____

5. You have finished this book, *One Faith, One Lord*. Explain one thing you have learned that will help you to be a better follower of Jesus Christ.

_____

_____

Vocation: Called to Serve

"Each of you has a special mission in life, and you each are called to be a disciple of Christ. Many of you will serve God in the vocation of Christian married life; some of you will serve him as dedicated single persons; some as priests and religious. But all of you must be the light of the world. To those of you who think that Christ may be inviting you to follow him in the priesthood or the consecrated life I make this personal appeal: I ask you to open your hearts generously to him; do not delay your response. The Lord will help you to know his will; he will help you to follow your vocation courageously."

Blessed Pope John Paul II
Youth Gathering in St. Louis, Missouri
January 26, 1999

What does the pope mean by "special mission" and "vocation"? Through the Sacrament of Baptism, we all share a mission or common vocation "to be the light of the world." We are called to show others Christ's love by our words and actions, to bring Christ to those who do not know him, and to grow in holiness. But God calls each of us to serve him in a personal and special way, too. This calling is our vocation. A vocation is more than a job we may have or a career we may pursue. A vocation is a calling to a particular way of life through which we can best love and serve God and others.

A vocation is a state of life—a way of living. For most of us discovering our vocation is a gradual process of prayer and questioning in which we are guided by the Holy Spirit and helped by others. This process is called discernment because we are trying to recognize, or discern, God's will for us. When we respond to God and fulfill our particular vocation, we become the person God wants us to be. We use our gifts and talents in ways that make us happy and bring happiness to others. God calls each one of us to serve him in one of the following particular vocations: laity, ordained ministry, or consecrated life.

The laity, or the Christian faithful, are members of the Church who share in the mission to bring the Good News of Christ to the world. All Catholics begin their lives as members of the laity. Many remain members of the laity for their entire lives, following God's call either in marriage or the single life. Marriage provides women and men the opportunity to share God's love with a spouse and to express that love by having children and bringing them up in a loving family. Each family is called to be a domestic Church, "a church in the home." Those called to the single life have the opportunity to share God's message and love through service to the community and the Church. Whether called to the single life or to marriage, women and men can respond to God's call by being active members of their families, parishes, and larger communities.

God calls some baptized men to serve him in the ordained ministry. Through the Sacrament of Holy Orders they are consecrated to the ministerial priesthood as priests and bishops, or to the permanent diaconate. Priests and bishops are ordained to serve the community through teaching, worship, and leadership.

There are two different types of priests: diocesan priests and religious priests. Diocesan

O Lord, help me know your will
for me.
Let your light shine in the depths
of my heart
that I may know what you want
me to do with my life.
Help me believe that you have
a special plan for me.
Lord, I know I pass through this
life only once;
help me decide how you want
me to make a difference.
Like our Blessed Mother, give me
the wisdom to hear your voice
and the courage to answer
your call.
Above all give me peace
of mind and heart.
I offer this prayer in the name of
Jesus Christ our Lord.
Amen.

priests are called to serve in a particular diocese. They help the bishop of that diocese by ministering in parishes. They also may assist in schools, hospitals, and prisons depending upon the local needs. Diocesan priests promise to lead a celibate life, not to marry. They also promise to respect and obey their bishop.

Religious priests are called to a specific religious order or congregation, such as the Franciscans, Dominicans, or Jesuits. These priests follow a religious rule, or plan of life, adopted by their founder.

Religious priests and some women and men who are not ordained are also called to the religious, or consecrated, life. Women religious are known as sisters, or nuns, and male religious who are not ordained as priests are known as brothers. They are involved in a variety of ministries of service to the Church.

Religious priests and religious women and men usually live in community and serve anywhere in the world that they are needed. They take the vows of poverty, chastity, and obedience. By these vows they pledge to own nothing of their own, to live a celibate life, and to be faithful and obedient to their superiors and the Church.

What is a Permanent Deacon?

A deacon is an ordained male minister of the Church who can preach, baptize, witness marriages, and preside at burials. Deacons assist the priest at Mass in ways such as reading the Gospel, preparing the altar, and distributing Holy Communion. Permanent deacons are often married and have an occupation or career to support themselves. A deacon is a sign of the service to which all Christians are called. Deacons do receive the Sacrament of Holy Orders, but they are ordained to assist the bishops and priests and to serve the whole Church. Deacons are not ministers of the Sacraments of Confirmation, Eucharist, Penance, Anointing of the Sick, and Holy Orders.

VOCATION

Celebrating the Seven Sacraments

Symbols of Sacraments	Why Do We Celebrate?	Who Is the Ordinary Minister?	What Elements Are Used?
BAPTISM	We are freed from sin, given the gift of God's life (grace), and become members of the Church.	bishop, priest, or deacon	water, holy oils, white garment, Easter candle, white candle for newly-baptized
CONFIRMATION	We are sealed with the Gift of the Holy Spirit and are strengthened.	bishop	Chrism for anointing
EUCHARIST	We are nourished with Christ's own Body and Blood. The Church fulfills the command of Jesus at the Last Supper to "do this in memory of me."	priest or bishop	bread and wine
PENANCE	We repent for our sins, and we are reconciled with God and the Church.	priest or bishop	stole
ANOINTING OF THE SICK	The seriously ill and/or the elderly are strengthened and comforted.	priest or bishop	Oil of the Sick for anointing
HOLY ORDERS	Baptized men are ordained deacons, priests, and bishops to serve as God's ministers to the Church.	bishop	Chrism for anointing; vestments for newly-ordained
MATRIMONY	A man and a woman commit themselves to each other and are blessed to carry out the responsibilities of marriage in mutual and lasting fidelity.	man and woman being married	wedding ring(s)

What Do We See?	What Do We Hear?	What Does the Community Do?
Pouring of water over forehead or immersion in baptismal pool; the putting on of the baptismal garment; presentation of candle lit from Easter Candle.	"(Name), I baptize you in the name of the Father, and of the Son, and of the Holy Spirit."	Renew baptismal promises; pray for and welcome new members.
Laying on of hand simultaneously with anointing on forehead; sponsor or godparent places right hand on candidate's shoulder.	"(Name), be sealed with the Gift of the Holy Spirit."	Renew baptismal promises; pray for newly-confirmed and give witness to their faith.
Celebrant or extraordinary minister of Holy Communion offers each communicant the Body and Blood of Christ.	"The Body of Christ." "Amen." "The Blood of Christ." "Amen."	Listen to the Word of God and respond, "Thanks be to God." Sing, pray, share the Sign of Peace. Receive Holy Communion. Go forth to love and serve the Lord.
Sign of the Cross by penitent at beginning of celebration and at absolution; priest extends right hand or both hands over head of penitent in absolution.	"…and I absolve you from your sins in the name of the Father, and of the Son, and of the Holy Spirit."	Experience and proclaim the mercy of God in their own lives; celebrate the Church's ongoing mission of reconciliation.
Anointing of the sick on their foreheads and hands; laying on of hands on heads of those who are ill.	"Through this holy anointing may the Lord in his love and mercy help you with the grace of the Holy Spirit. May the Lord who frees you from sin save you and raise you up."	Celebrate the sacrament with those who are sick; do all they can to help the sick return to health.
Laying on of hands; anointing of the hands of newly-ordained priests.	(For priests): "Almighty Father, grant this servant of yours the dignity of the priesthood. Renew within him the spirit of holiness…."	Pray that the gifts of Heaven will be poured out on the candidate; support him in his ministry.
Joining of right hands by the man and woman; exchange of rings; blessing of bride and groom.	"I, (name), take you, [name], to be my wife [husband]. I promise to be true to you in good times and in bad, in sickness and in health. I will love you and honor you all the days of my life."	Celebrate with the bride and groom; support them in prayer and witness.

THE SEVEN SACRAMENTS

115

✝ The Church's Liturgical Year ✝

The liturgical year is the name we give to the Church's year. It is our way of celebrating the mystery of Christ as we move from day to day and season to season. Throughout the liturgical year we proclaim and celebrate the different aspects of the mystery of Christ.

The major parts of the Church's year are the seasons: Advent, Christmas, Lent, the Easter Triduum, Easter, and Ordinary Time. Centered around the great feast of the Easter Triduum, the seasons enable us to walk with Jesus once again through his birth, his life on earth, his suffering, Death, Resurrection, and Ascension.

In the Mass and in the Liturgy of the Hours, we rejoice daily in God's presence and power in the world. Priests pray the Liturgy of the Hours as part of their ministry. Some parishes celebrate part of the Liturgy of the Hours called Evening Prayer so that all can join in marking the hour as blessed by God. In monasteries, religious men and women traditionally pray the Liturgy of the Hours at seven different times during the day and night.

Sundays are the heart of our weekly liturgical cycle. Each Sunday we celebrate that Jesus rose from the dead on the first day of the week. Also known as the Lord's Day, Sunday is a time to rest from work, to enjoy God's gift of Creation and family, and to serve those in need.

Feast days mark the liturgical year with celebrations of special events in the lives of Jesus, Mary, and the saints. These celebrations help us to remember that we belong to the Communion of Saints who intercede for us in Heaven.

Advent
Advent is the beginning of our liturgical year. It is the time of preparation for both the celebration of the Lord's first coming at his birth and his second coming at the end of time. The Advent season begins four Sundays before December 25 and ends at the Christmas Eve Vigil Mass.

The traditional color of the vestments and decorations for the days of Advent is purple. It signifies that this is a time of expectation.

Christmas
This season celebrates Jesus' birth and the joyous events associated with it. It is the period from Jesus' birth to the beginning of his public ministry. The Christmas season begins at the Christmas Eve Vigil Mass and ends on the Feast of the Baptism of the Lord.

The primary color of the vestments for this season is white. Gold is also used. These colors signify our joy at the presence of Christ with us.

Lent
The season of Lent begins on Ash Wednesday. During Lent we remember that Jesus suffered, died, and rose to new life to save us from sin and to give us new life in the Kingdom of God. During Lent we work to grow closer to Jesus and to one another through prayer, fasting, and almsgiving. We pray for and support all who are preparing for the Sacraments of Christian Initiation. We prepare for the Easter Triduum. The color for Lent is purple, for penance.

The Easter Triduum
The Easter Triduum is the Church's greatest and most important celebration. The word *triduum* means "three days." During the three days of the Easter Triduum—from Holy Thursday evening, through Good Friday and Holy Saturday, until Easter Sunday evening—we remember and celebrate in the liturgy, with many special traditions and rituals, the suffering, Death, and Resurrection of Jesus Christ. The color for Good Friday is red, for Jesus' suffering. The color for the other days of the Triduum is white.

Easter
The season of Easter begins on Easter Sunday evening and continues until Pentecost Sunday, 50 days later. During this season we rejoice in Jesus' Resurrection and in the new life we have in Jesus Christ. We also celebrate Christ's Ascension into Heaven. The color for the Easter season is white, while Pentecost's color is red and signifies the descent of the Holy Spirit upon the Apostles.

Ordinary Time
During this season we remember and celebrate the teaching, stories, and events of Jesus' life. The emphasis on these Sundays is on the celebration of and instruction in our Christian faith and morals.

The periods of this season occur between the Christmas and Lenten seasons and after the Easter season until Advent. The liturgical color of this season is green, a sign of life and hope.

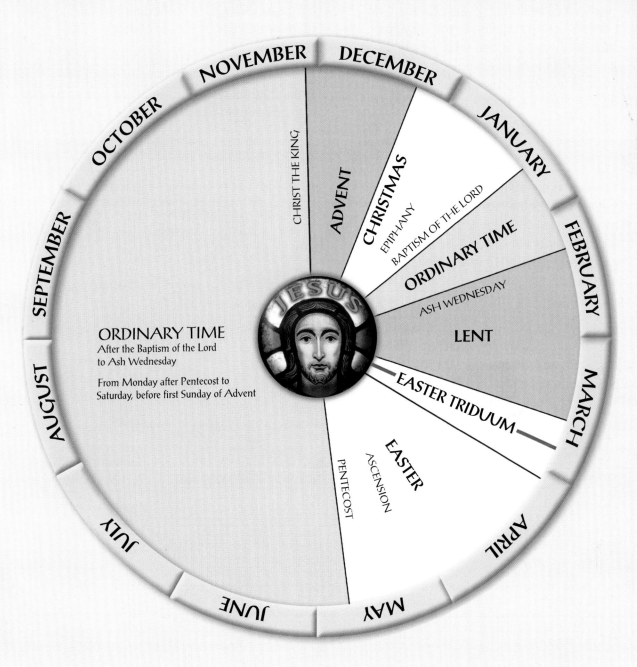

ORDINARY TIME

After the Baptism of the Lord
to Ash Wednesday

From Monday after Pentecost to
Saturday, before first Sunday of Advent

Wheel labels (outer ring, clockwise): NOVEMBER · DECEMBER · JANUARY · FEBRUARY · MARCH · APRIL · MAY · JUNE · JULY · AUGUST · SEPTEMBER · OCTOBER

Wheel labels (inner seasons): CHRIST THE KING · ADVENT · CHRISTMAS · EPIPHANY · BAPTISM OF THE LORD · ORDINARY TIME · ASH WEDNESDAY · LENT · EASTER TRIDUUM · EASTER · ASCENSION · PENTECOST · JESUS

**U.S. Holy Days of Obligation celebrated
by the Church in the United States:**

Solemnity of Mary, Mother of God (January 1)

Ascension (when celebrated on Thursday during
the Easter season)*

Assumption of Mary (August 15)

All Saints' Day (November 1)

Immaculate Conception (December 8)

Christmas (December 25)

*(Most dioceses celebrate the Ascension on the following Sunday.)

LITURGICAL YEAR

Using the Bible

The Bible is a collection of seventy-three books written under the inspiration of the Holy Spirit. The Bible is divided into two parts, The Old Testament and the New Testament. In the forty-six books of the Old Testament, we learn about the story of God's relationship with the people of Israel. In the twenty-seven books of the New Testament, we learn about the story of Jesus Christ, the Son of God, and of his followers.

Because God inspired the human authors of the individual books of the Bible, he is the author of the Bible. That is why in the Liturgy of the Word at Mass the reader concludes a reading by saying, "The Word of the Lord" to which we respond, "Thanks be to God." We are grateful that we have received the Word of God and it is at work in us.

When we read the Bible with attention and respect, we are praying. The Word of God, written down by human authors under the inspiration of the Holy Spirit, enters our hearts and minds. The Holy Spirit enables us to be attentive to what God has revealed through these authors.

The Word of God moves us to become more loving, truthful, forgiving, and compassionate. It strengthens our faith, increases our understanding, and guides us in making good decisions.

One way to use the Bible in prayer is to follow these simple steps:

- Pray for the help of the Holy Spirit.

- Choose one story or teaching of Jesus and read it slowly to yourself.

- Read it again aloud.

- Focus on one or two verses that are especially meaningful to you.

- Ask the Holy Spirit to guide you in living by your chosen verses.

- Thank God for the Word that is living and active in you.

How to Find Your Way in the Bible

Matthew, 13   28

The Demand for a Sign 38 r*Then some of the scribes and Pharisees said to him, "Teacher, we wish to see a sign from you." 39*He said to them in reply, "An evil and unfaithful generation seeks a sign, but no sign will be given it except the sign of Jonah the prophet. 40*Just as Jonah was in the belly of the whale three days and three nights, so will the Son of Man be in the heart of the earth three days and three nights. 41*At the judgment, the men of Nineveh will arise with this generation and condemn it, because they repented at the preaching of Jonah; and there is something greater than Jonah here. 42 s At the judgment the queen of the south will arise with this generation and condemn it, because she came from the ends of the earth to hear the wisdom of Solomon; and there is something greater than Solomon here.

The Return of the Unclean Spirit 43 t*"When an unclean spirit goes out of a person it roams through arid regions searching for rest but finds none. 44Then it says, 'I will return to my home from which I came.' But upon returning, it finds it empty, swept clean, and put in order. 45Then it

goes and brings back with itself seven other spirits more evil than itself, and they move in and dwell there; and the last condition of that person is worse than the first. Thus it will be with this evil generation."

The True Family of Jesus 46 u*While he was still speaking to the crowds, his mother and his brothers appeared outside, wishing to speak with him. [47*Someone told him, "Your mother and your brothers are standing outside, asking to speak with you."] 48But he said in reply to the one who told him, "Who is my mother? Who are my brothers?" 49And stretching out his hand toward his disciples, he said, "Here are my mother and my brothers. 50For whoever does the will of my heavenly Father is my brother, and sister, and mother."

CHAPTER 13

The Parable of the Sower 1 v*On that day, Jesus went out of the house and sat down by the sea. 2Such large crowds gathered around him that he got into a boat and sat down, and the whole crowd stood along the shore. 3*And he

Book of the Bible
Each book is divided into chapters, and each chapter into verses.

Verse number

Verse (Matthew 12:38)

Passage title
Titles added to break up the chapters, not actual words of the Bible.

Passage (Matthew 12:46–50)
A section of a chapter made up of a number of verses.

The Bible reference Matthew 12:46–50 means: the Gospel (book) of Matthew, chapter twelve, verses forty-six to fifty.

Chapter number

Sign of the Cross

In the name of the Father,
and of the Son,
and of the Holy Spirit.
Amen.

Glory to the Father

Glory to the Father,
and to the Son,
and to the Holy Spirit:
as it was in the beginning,
is now, and will be for ever.
Amen.

Our Father

Our Father, who art in heaven,
hallowed be thy name;
thy kingdom come;
thy will be done on earth
as it is in heaven.
Give us this day our daily bread;
and forgive us our trespasses
as we forgive those
who trespass against us;
and lead us not into temptation,
but deliver us from evil.
Amen.

Apostles' Creed

I believe in God,
the Father almighty,
Creator of heaven and earth,
and in Jesus Christ, his only Son, our Lord,
who was conceived by the Holy Spirit,
born of the Virgin Mary,
suffered under Pontius Pilate,
was crucified, died and was buried;
he descended into hell;
on the third day he rose again from the dead;
he ascended into heaven,
and is seated at the right hand of God the
Father almighty;
from there he will come to judge
the living and the dead.

I believe in the Holy Spirit,
the holy catholic Church,
the communion of saints,
the forgiveness of sins,
the resurrection of the body,
and life everlasting.
Amen.

Hail Mary

Hail Mary, full of grace,
the Lord is with you!
Blessed are you among women,
and blessed is the fruit
of your womb, Jesus.
Holy Mary, Mother of God,
pray for us sinners,
now and at the hour of our death.
Amen.

Nicene Creed

I believe in one God,
the Father almighty,
maker of heaven and earth,
of all things visible and invisible.

I believe in one Lord Jesus Christ,
the Only Begotten Son of God,
born of the Father before all ages.
God from God, Light from Light,
true God from true God,
begotten, not made, consubstantial
with the Father;
through him all things were made.
For us men and for our salvation
he came down from heaven,
and by the Holy Spirit was incarnate of
   the Virgin Mary,
and became man.

For our sake he was crucified
   under Pontius Pilate,
he suffered death and was buried,
and rose again on the third day
in accordance with the Scriptures.
He ascended into heaven
and is seated at the right hand of the
   Father.
He will come again in glory
to judge the living and the dead
and his kingdom will have no end.

I believe in the Holy Spirit, the Lord,
   the giver of life,
who proceeds from the Father and the
   Son,
who with the Father and the Son is
   adored and glorified,
who has spoken through the prophets.

I believe in one, holy, catholic and
   apostolic Church.
I confess one Baptism for the
   forgiveness of sins
and I look forward to the resurrection
   of the dead
and the life of the world to come.
   Amen.

Prayer to the Holy Spirit

Come, Holy Spirit,
fill the hearts of your faithful.
And kindle in them the fire of your love.
Send forth your Spirit and they shall be created.
And you will renew the face of the earth.
   Amen.

A Morning Prayer

God our Father,
work is your gift to us,
a call to reach new heights
by using our talents for the good of all.
Guide us as we work and teach us to live
in the spirit that has made us your sons
   and daughters,
in the love that has made us brothers
   and sisters.
Grant this through Christ our Lord.
   Amen.

An Evening Prayer

Lord God,
send peaceful sleep
to refresh our tired bodies.
May your help always renew us
and keep us strong in your service.
We ask this through Christ our Lord.
   Amen.

Grace Before Meals

Bless us, O Lord,
and these your gifts
which we are about to receive
from your goodness.
Through Christ our Lord.
Amen.

Grace After Meals

We give you thanks for all your gifts,
almighty God,
living and reigning now and for ever.
Amen.

Act of Contrition

My God,
I am sorry for my sins
with all my heart.
In choosing to do wrong
and failing to do good,
I have sinned against you
whom I should love above all things.
I firmly intend, with your help,
to do penance,
to sin no more,
and to avoid whatever leads me to sin.
Our Savior Jesus Christ
suffered and died for us.
In his name, my God, have mercy.
Amen.

Hail, Holy Queen

Hail, Holy Queen, mother of mercy,
hail, our life, our sweetness,
and our hope.
To you we cry, the children of Eve;
to you we send up our sighs,
mourning and weeping in this land of exile.
Turn, then, most gracious advocate,
your eyes of mercy toward us;
lead us home at last
and show us the blessed fruit
of your womb, Jesus:
O clement, O loving, O sweet Virgin Mary!
Amen.

The Jesus Prayer

Lord Jesus Christ, Son of God, have mercy
on me, a sinner.
Amen.

Prayer of Saint Francis

Lord, make me an instrument of
your peace:
where there is hatred, let me sow love;
where there is injury, pardon;
where there is doubt, faith;
where there is despair, hope;
where there is darkness, light;
where there is sadness, joy.

O Divine Master, grant that I may not
so much seek
to be consoled as to console,
to be understood as to understand,
to be loved as to love.

For it is in giving that we receive,
it is in pardoning that we are pardoned,
it is in dying that we are born to
eternal life.
Amen.

Christian life is nourished through the liturgy. It is also nourished by various devotions and practices.

Sacramentals are holy objects, actions, and blessings used by the Church and in private devotions. They help us recognize the sacredness of our lives. Among the most common sacramental objects are rosaries, medals, holy water, holy oil, candles, and blessed ashes and palms.

The Rosary

The rosary combines vocal and meditative prayer in which we consider the joyful, the sorrowful, the glorious, and the luminous mysteries in the lives of Jesus and Mary. Begin with the Sign of the Cross. Pray the Apostles' Creed. Then pray one Our Father on the first bead after the cross on the rosary. Follow this by three Hail Marys on the next three beads. Pray one Glory to the Father.

To pray each decade, or group of ten beads, begin with the Our Father on the larger bead and follow with ten Hail Marys on the smaller beads. Close each decade with a Glory to the Father. As you pray, consider in your heart the particular mystery or special event in the lives of Jesus and Mary. At the end of the rosary, pray the Hail, Holy Queen.

The Mysteries of the Rosary

The Joyful Mysteries

1. The Annunciation
2. The Visitation
3. The Birth of Jesus
4. The Presentation of Jesus in the Temple
5. The Finding of Jesus in the Temple

The Sorrowful Mysteries

1. The Agony in the Garden
2. The Scourging at the Pillar
3. The Crowning with Thorns
4. The Carrying of the Cross
5. The Crucifixion and Death of Jesus

The Glorious Mysteries

1. The Resurrection
2. The Ascension
3. The Descent of the Holy Spirit upon the Apostles
4. The Assumption of Mary into Heaven
5. The Coronation of Mary as Queen of Heaven

The Luminous Mysteries

1. Jesus' Baptism in the Jordan
2. The Miracle at the Wedding at Cana
3. Jesus Announces the Kingdom of God
4. The Transfiguration
5. The Institution of the Eucharist

The Stations of the Cross

From the earliest of days of the Church, Christians remembered Jesus' life and Death by visiting and praying at the places where Jesus lived, suffered, died, and rose from the dead.

As the Church spread to other countries, not everyone could travel to the Holy Land. So local churches began inviting people to "follow in the footsteps of Jesus" without leaving home. "Stations," or places to stop and pray, were made so that stay-at-home pilgrims could "walk the way of the cross" in their own parish churches. We do the same today, especially during Lent.

There are fourteen "stations," or stops. At each one, we pause and think about what is happening at the station. Then we pray:

We adore you, O Christ,
and we bless you,
Because by your holy cross,
you have redeemed the world.

Jesus is condemned to die.

Jesus takes up his cross.

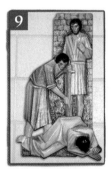
Jesus falls the first time.

Jesus meets his mother.

Simon helps Jesus carry his cross.

Veronica wipes the face of Jesus.

Jesus falls the second time.

Jesus meets the women of Jerusalem.

Jesus falls the third time.

Jesus is stripped of his garments.

Jesus is nailed to the cross.

Jesus dies on the cross.

Jesus is taken down from the cross.

Jesus is laid in the tomb.

Prayer before reading Scripture

"Your word is a lamp for my feet,
   a light for my path." (Psalm 119:105)

Blessing and Giving of Ashes

On Ash Wednesday, the first day of Lent, we are marked with ashes on our foreheads in the Sign of the Cross. Ashes are a sign of sorrow for sin and a reminder of death.

"Remember that you are dust,
   and unto dust you shall return."
      (See Genesis 3:19)

Blessing and Giving of Palms

On Passion, or Palm, Sunday at the beginning of Holy Week, the Church distributes blessed palm branches to everyone at Mass. We hold the palms during the Gospel reading in honor of Jesus who was greeted by a crowd bearing palm branches when he entered Jerusalem in triumph on the Sabbath before his suffering and Death.

"Hosanna to the Son of David;
   blessed is he who comes
      in the name of the Lord;
   hosanna in the highest." (Matthew 21:9)

Visit to the Most Blessed Sacrament

Catholics believe that Jesus is truly present in our churches in the Most Blessed Sacrament. The Eucharist is kept in a tabernacle as Holy Communion for the sick and for adoration. The Church encourages us to visit the Most Blessed Sacrament out of gratitude and as an expression of our love and adoration for Jesus Christ. We genuflect or bow to the tabernacle, enter a nearby pew or row, and take a few minutes to share our love, our hopes, our needs, and our thanks with Jesus.

Making a Pilgrimage

Pilgrimages provide special occasions for growth and renewal in prayer. Christians join together to journey to shrines or other holy places for prayer, reconciliation, and the celebration of Eucharist. Often all or part of the journey is made on foot.

"Happy are those who find refuge in you,
   whose hearts are set on pilgrim roads."
      (Psalm 84:6)

"Pray without ceasing."
   (1 Thessalonians 5:17)

Advocate a title of the Holy Spirit, the third Person of the Blessed Trinity

Annunciation the announcement to Mary that she would be the mother of the Son of God

Apostles the twelve men chosen by Jesus to share in his mission in a special way

apostolic succession the name given to describe the Apostles' authority and call to service that has been handed down to their successors, the pope and bishops

Assumption the truth that at the end of her earthly life, God brought Mary body and soul to Heaven to live forever with the risen Jesus

Baptism the first and foundational sacrament by which we become sharers in God's divine life, are freed from Original Sin and all personal sins, become children of God, and are welcomed into the Church

Beatitudes teachings that describe how to live as Jesus' disciples

Bible the written account of God's Revelation and his relationship with his people

Blessed Trinity the three Divine Persons in one God: God the Father, God the Son, and God the Holy Spirit

Catholic social teaching the teaching of the Church that calls all members to work for justice and peace as Jesus did

charity the gift from God that enables us to love him above all things and to love our neighbor as ourselves

chastity the virtue that is a gift from God which calls us to use our human sexuality in a responsible and faithful way

Church the community of people who believe in Jesus Christ, have been baptized in him, and follow his teachings

Communion of Saints the union of all the baptized members of the Church on earth, in Heaven, and in Purgatory

Confirmation the sacrament in which we receive the Gift of the Holy Spirit in a special way

conscience our ability to know the difference between good and evil, right and wrong

diocese a local area of the Church led by a bishop

disciple one who says yes to Jesus' call to follow him

Divine Inspiration the special guidance that the Holy Spirit gave to the human authors of the Bible

Divine Revelation God's making himself known to us

Ecumenical Councils meetings of the pope and bishops to discuss and make decisions on issues of faith, morals, and life of the Church

Eucharist the Sacrament of the Body and Blood of Christ, who is truly present under the appearance of bread and wine

eucharistic fast abstaining from food or drink (other than water and medicine) for one hour before receiving Holy Communion

Eucharistic Prayer the center of the celebration of the Mass and the heart of the Catholic faith; the great prayer of thanksgiving and Consecration

Evangelization the sharing of the Good News of Jesus Christ and the love of God with all people, in every circumstance of life

faith the gift from God by which we believe in God and all that he has revealed, and all that the Church proposes for our belief

Gifts of the Holy Spirit seven special gifts that help us to live as faithful followers and true witnesses of Jesus Christ: wisdom, understanding, counsel, fortitude, knowledge, piety, and fear of the Lord

Gospels the accounts found in the New Testament of God's Revelation through Jesus Christ

grace a participation, or sharing, in God's life and friendship

Heaven the ultimate happiness of living with God forever

Hell the state of everlasting separation from God because of lack of contrition for and absolution from mortal sin

hope the gift from God by which we desire eternal life, place our trust in Christ's promises, and rely on the help of the Holy Spirit

human dignity the value and worth we share because God created us in his image and likeness

Immaculate Conception the truth that God preserved Mary from Original Sin and all sin from the very moment she was conceived

Incarnation the truth that the Son of God, the second Person of the Blessed Trinity, became man and lived among us in order to accomplish our Salvation

Kingdom of God the power of God's love active in our lives and in our world. It is present now and will come in its fullness at the end of time.

Last Judgment Jesus Christ's coming at the end of time to judge all people

Lectionary the book containing all the readings that we use during the Liturgy of the Word at Mass; it is not the whole Bible but a collection of parts of the Bible arranged for reading at Mass

liturgy the official public prayer of the Church

Marks of the Church the four characteristics of the Church: one, holy, catholic, and apostolic

Mass the Church's great prayer of praise and thanks to God the Father; the celebration of the Eucharist

Messiah the person God planned to send to save people from their sins. Jesus Christ is the Messiah because as Savior he fulfilled God's promise.

modesty the virtue by which we dress, act, speak, and think in ways that show respect for ourselves and others

mortal sin very serious sin that turns us completely away from God because it is a choice we freely make to do something that we know is seriously wrong

New Commandment Jesus' summary of all of his teachings on love: "Love one another. As I have loved you, so you also should love one another. This is how all will know that you are my disciples, if you have love for one another" (John 13: 34–35).

New Testament the second part of the Bible consisting of twenty-seven books about Jesus Christ, the Son of God, his message and mission, and his first followers

Old Testament the first part of the Bible consisting of forty-six books. In them we read about the faith relationship between God and the Israelites, later called the Jews

Original Sin the first sin committed by the first human beings

parish the community of believers who worship and work together

Paschal Mystery the suffering, Death, Resurrection, and Ascension of Jesus Christ

Passover the feast on which Jewish people remember the miraculous way that God saved them from death and slavery in ancient Egypt

pastor the priest who leads the parish in worship, prayer, and teaching

Pentecost the day on which the Holy Spirit came to Jesus' first disciples as Jesus promised

prayer the raising of our minds and hearts to God

Precepts of the Church laws of the Church that help us to see that loving God and others is connected to a life of prayer, worship, and service

Purgatory a process of purification after death for a person who has sinned; those experiencing Purgatory are certain of Heaven

Real Presence the true presence of Jesus Christ in the Eucharist under the appearance of bread and wine

Resurrection the mystery of Jesus' rising from Death to new life

Sacrament of Penance and Reconciliation sacrament by which our relationship with God and the Church is restored and our sins are forgiven

sacraments effective signs given to us by Jesus Christ through which we share in God's life

sin a thought, word, deed, or omission against God's law that harms us and our relationship with God and others

soul the invisible spiritual reality that makes each of us human and that will never die

stewards of Creation those who take care of everything that God has given them

Ten Commandments laws of God's covenant given to Moses on Mount Sinai

theological virtues the virtues of faith, hope, and charity, which have God as their source, motive, and object

Tradition the living transmission of the Word of God as entrusted to the Apostles and their successors by Jesus Christ and the Holy Spirit

venial sin less serious sin that weakens our friendship with God but does not turn us completely away from him

virtue a good habit that helps a person to act according to reason and faith

witnesses people who speak and act based upon what they know and believe about Jesus Christ

Works of Mercy acts of love by which we care for the bodily and spiritual needs of others

Italicized numbers refer to definitions. **Bold-faced** numbers refer to chapters.

Index

Italicized numbers refer to definitions. **Bold-faced** numbers refer to chapters.